COOKING WITH THE LODGE CAST IRON SKILLET COOKBOOK

BEST Essential Family Meals and My Easy at Home Non Stick Oven Pan Recipes for You to Enjoy

A.J. LUIGI

Cooking with the Lodge Cast Iron Skillet Cookbook

LEGAL:

DISCLAIMER: This book is independently published by, and is **not** affiliated with, sponsored by, or endorsed by any of the products mentioned in this book. All other company and product names are the trademarks of their respective owners.

This information contained in this book is for entertainment purposes only. The content represents the opinion of the author and is based on the author's personal experience and observations. The author does not assume any liability whatsoever for the use of or inability to use any or all information contained in this book, and accepts no responsibility for any loss or damages of any kind that may be incurred by the reader as a result of actions arising from the use of the information in this book. Use this information at your own risk. No part of this book may be reproduced or transmitted in any form or by any means, electronic or mechanical, including photocopying, recording, or by any information storage or retrieval system, without express written permission from the author, except in the case of brief quotations embodied in critical articles and reviews – or except by a reviewer who may quote brief passages in a review.

Respective authors hold all copyrights not held by the publisher

NOTE: Some of the recipes in this book include raw eggs. Raw eggs may contain bacteria. It is recommended that you purchase certified salmonella-free eggs from a reliable source and store them in the refrigerator. You should not feed raw eggs to babies or small kids. Likewise, pregnant women, elderly persons, or those with a compromised immune system should not eat raw eggs. Neither the author nor the publisher claims responsibility for adverse effects resulting from the use of the recipes and/or information found within this book.

The author reserves the right to make any changes he or she deems necessary to future versions of the publication to ensure its accuracy.

COPYRIGHT © 2018 Recipe Nerds All Rights Reserved.
Published in The United States of America by Recipe Nerds.

www.RecipeNerds.com | Facebook.com/RecipeNerds

A.J. Luigi

INTRODUCTION:

Well, let's speak some truth about the "Cast Iron Cookware!" It has outlasted all cookware and is still the best cooking you could ever do. Because of the way it holds heat will make you look like a pro every time you use it to cook in your kitchen. We have put together this book to show you the new creative way to use your cast iron for cooking. We have our mouth-watering recipes to give you and your family something to crave! All of our Professional Chefs have pulled together to give some of their deepest secrets as far as "Cast Iron Cooking" deliciousness!

We used a few of the Lodge Cast Iron Skillets to come up with some of the BEST RECIPES that were inspired from top restaurants across the globe! The various recipe sections in this book will make you crave more after every meal! These meals that we have prepared are simple to make, easy to read and delicious to eat! If you are cooking for that special someone, we will show you how to impress them with some of our "Pro Tips." It could be just as easy as topping that meal with an elegant garnish! These are simple restaurant techniques that are used in all high-end restaurants that make you say "Wow!"
So, come on and dive in to these succulent recipes and see what else you can make for your friends and family!

We have poured our hearts into this book for you, and have a section in the back for you to write some of your very own cast iron creations in the back of this (your very own) personal book. Simple, easy and delicious recipes for you to enjoy with everyone!

Hope you enjoy!
With a warm heart...

A.J. Luigi, Professional Chef

Cooking with the Lodge Cast Iron Skillet Cookbook

TABLE OF CONTENTS

Legal:	2
Introduction:	3
Table of Contents	4
More Than Just a Piece of Iron!	8
It's a bird! No, it's a plane! No...what IS that?!	8
Why Cast Iron is *Better* for Cooking	8
Seasoned, or Not Seasoned? That is the Question!	10
Stovetop, Oven or Grill! You Have Options!	12
The Possibilities are Endless!	13
What NOT to Cook in Cast Iron	18
Any Meal...All in ONE Pan!	19
Better Than Grandma's Cooking	20
The Magic is in the Skillet	21
The Sizzling Reason Doctors Want You Using Cast Iron	21
Hot as a Two-Dollar Pistol (Heat Distribution)	23
Handle with Care	23
Caring for Your Cast Iron Skillet	25
Easy Cleaning	26
Restoring Cast Iron	27
Cast Iron Skillet Sins	28
Pro Tips from the Chef!	30
The Pro Way to Season Your Cast Iron	30
Cast Iron Pro Cooking Tips	32
Conclusion	33

Yours for Looking — 34
"BONUS" Get Your Marinades for Meats & Veggies! — 34

Best Beef: — 35
Cast Iron Oven Baked Beef Stew — 36
Cast Iron Skillet Nachos — 37
Montana Style Cowboy Skillet Steak — 38
Broccoli Beef — 39
Ground Beef Shepard's Pie — 40
Cheesy Skillet Hamburgers — 41
Beefy, Cheesy Skillet Lasagna — 42

Pulsating Poultry: — 43
Comfort Skillet Chicken Pot Pie — 44
Sweet Potato and Savory Ground Turkey Skillet — 45
Chicken Sausage with Basil and Gnocchi — 46
Skillet Roasted Chicken — 47
Skillet Tangy Lemon Turkey — 48
Prosciutto Wrapped Skillet Seared Chicken — 49

Fantastic Fish: — 50
Buttery Tarragon Encrusted Seared Salmon — 51
Zesty Shrimp and Crab Bake — 52
Korean Tuna Cakes — 53
Creole Style Grouper — 54
Spanish Skillet Tilapia — 55
Herb Blackened Trout — 56

Perfected Pork: — 57
One Skillet Pork Cacciatore — 58
Cast Iron Skillet Fried Ham Steak — 59
Pork Tenderloin with Vegetable Medley — 60
Sizzling Spicy New Mexico Ham Steak — 61
Bacon Wrapped Pork — 62
Slow Roasted Skillet Pork Roast — 63

Cooking with the Lodge Cast Iron Skillet Cookbook

Very Vegetarian:	64
Tomato Basil Skillet Pizza	65
Skillet Corn Casserole	66
Tomato and Caprese Grilled Cheese	67
Bean and Cheese Skillet Quesadillas	68
Cast Iron Skillet Brussels Sprouts Orecchiette	69
Vegan Hamburger Helper	70

Succulent Sides:	71
Spinach and Potato Hash	72
One Cast Iron Skillet Zesty Salsa	73
Creamy Chicken Soup Mac & Cheese	74
Skillet Fried Okra	75
Honeyed White Turnips	76
Skillet Garlic Sweet Potatoes	77

Bring Home Breakfast:	78
Egg and Tater Tot Breakfast Pizza	79
Easy Weekday Morning Skillet Breakfast	80
Berry Skillet Cakes	81
The Best Scrambled Egg Recipe	82
Cinnamon-Vanilla French toast	83
Hearty Breakfast Casserole	84

Delicious Desserts:	85
One Stop Skillet S'mores Graham Cracker Dip	86
Peanut Buttery Reese's Nachos	87
One Size Skillet Toffee Brownie	88
Caramel Giant Cinnamon Roll	89
Gooey Chocolatey Texas Skillet Cake	90
Brown Sugar and Butterscotch Skillet Pumpkin Pie	91

Next Up On the List!	92
Show Us Some Love… ☺	92

Yours for Looking — 93
"BONUS" Get Your Marinades for Meats & Veggies! — 93
Metric Volume Conversions Chart — 94
Metric Weight Conversion Chart — 95
Temperature Conversion Chart — 95

About The Author — 96
Cast Iron Skillet Secret Recipe Creations & Notes: — 97

MORE THAN JUST A PIECE OF IRON!

It's a bird! No, it's a plane! No...what IS that?!
While I hope that this highly indestructible kitchen tool would not be falling from the sky, I have no doubt that it would make the drop without a dent or scratch. Go try it if you think I am bluffing!

But really, this book is all about the bad boy of your kitchen, the cast iron skillet. Why have we created a book that highlights this old-as-time cooking utensil? Because with the creation of so many 'easy-to-use' (but hard to figure out) kitchen gadgets and appliances, items like this skillet in particular get thrown in the unwanted corner cabinet and forgotten. The truth is, no matter how many new-fangled gizmos are fabricated, the cast iron skillet will continue to stand the test of time!

Why Cast Iron is *Better* for Cooking
Even if you are on the fence about dusting off or finally purchasing a cast iron skillet, I bet after this section alone you will reconsider! There are many culinary and practical reason why cast iron has been making a solid comeback.

Enhances the more you use it
How many items in your kitchen can you say *improve* the more you use them? I will answer this question for you: little to none! Even after years of heavy usage, instead of wearing down and having to purchase a new one, it develops a slick, natural patina, known as seasoning, which allows food to come off its surface easier. In fact, well-seasoned skillets can be just as non-stick, if not more so than its stainless-steel and aluminum cousins.

Cultivates heat
While the cast iron skillet does have so issues with its ability to transfer heat to various parts of the metal, it can hold heat like a champ! Once your skillet is hot, it will stay that way for a long while, which is what makes it great for searing that tasty slab of steak. When you add a cold steak to the cast iron, a temperature drop occurs, which allows for higher heat and results in much better browning, which is essential to the perfect steak.

Practically immortal
What is so legendary about the cast iron skillet is its durability. This piece of kitchen equipment can easily be passed down among generations. Another great attribute is that it can very easily be restored if misused.

Safer than modern cookware
Cast iron skillets have been around for more than 2,000 years. WHOA. This means they've been used as a main source of cooking for like, ever. Even though it was created back in the good old days, it still ranks number one in safety among aluminum, earthenware, copper, stainless-steel, and non-stick pans.
Cast iron pans are the best for cooking over high heat since its coating protects the pan from coming in contact with what is being cooked. Iron is a mineral our body used, which means any additional iron that comes in contact with your meal will do the body no harm.

No need for additional oil
If you are one of those crazy folks who like to dabble in the latest and 'greatest' diet fads, then cooking with cast iron is a huge bonus because you only need a small amount of oil to cook with and don't have to consistently keep adding it like with other pans. Just a thin layer over the skillet's surface is all you need to ensure your meal is cooked properly without the risk of burning!

Seasoned, or Not Seasoned? That is the Question!

Cast iron skillets come in two styles: enamel-coated and bare.

Bare skillets
Bare is obvious; it is an unaltered skillet that is made with no covering to put them under the non-stick category. Bare skillets become reactive when they are heated and must be seasoned to use them and develop that much-desired patina if you wish for a non-stick skillet.

As you can imagine, bare skillets are cheaper and have more potential to be used for longer periods of time, which makes whatever number is on the price tag totally worth it.

Enamel and porcelain-coated

Enamel skillets are created to be non-stick right from the get-go and are known to be non-reactive to foods cooked inside it. These skillets do not need to be seasoned, but do require regular cleaning and care to keep the enamel finish intact.

If misused or not maintained properly, the coating will eventually wear off, which makes the skillet unusable. The enamel coating also comes at a loftier price than bare skillets, at around $150 for a porcelain coat. The quality of the coating with enamel cast iron version needs to be looked at closely before you buy it.

A battle of the skillets

Let me shed some truth to make your decision a little easier, however;
Cast iron skillets are meant to last most of your life here on planet Earth, if not longer. Choosing to invest in a cheap pan with a wild reputation to shed its coating is a solid waste of your hard-earned cash.

The coating needs to be thick and sustainable enough to get abused with cooking utensils and many various food, which still letting heat to pass through and be transferred. Your pan should be even with not one inch having a varying thickness from the next.

If you see an uneven coating application, put that pan back on the shelf for another sucker who is less educated than you in the world of cast iron to deal with. Uneven coating makes cooking challenging, if not impossible.

If you choose to buy enamel coated cast iron, be prepared to perform careful actions, such as discarding sharp, metal cooking utensils that could potentially scrape off the enamel finish and leave you with a pot that can no longer cook at the same temperature.

STOVETOP, OVEN OR GRILL! YOU HAVE OPTIONS!

OVEN   **STOVE TOP**   **GRILL**

Now to the chapter that is sure to make your mouth water and your taste buds *begging* you to get a cast iron skillet if you don't already have one. (Seriously, what are you waiting for? I can wait while you go to the store. No biggie!)

The best aspect of cooking with cast iron and why so many at home chefs swear by its use is because of its ability to stay screaming hot. Unlike aluminum and other thinner pans, heat does not fluctuate in cast iron, which makes it ideal for foods that cook and taste better at high heat. Good eatin' such as roasts and steaks that require you to brown before braising? Yeah, get yourself a cast iron skillet already!

When you are searing meat, the surface takes on that beautiful deep brown color and develops a crust without gaining those nasty black bits from the bottom of the pan. Can you say YUM. If you can't imagine yourself as a chef of your at-home kitchen, well, start to dream!

A.J. Luigi

The Possibilities are Endless!

Hold onto something sturdy, because your mind is about to be *blown* with the things you have been cooking wrong your entire life! Okay, maybe not wrong, but not *right* according to your taste buds!

Fried chicken
What?! No... no way! YES WAY. Leave that Fry Daddy under the counter because when compared to cast iron, nothing comes close. If you fail to believe me, check out blogs from chefs and food bloggers that are all in agreement that frying chicken in the cast iron skillet creates the most glorious, crunchified chicken EVER.

The secret? The ability to retain heat along with a small amount of oil. In fact, anything that is battered or requires to be fried can benefit from the heat-retaining magic of cast iron. Plus, each time you cook with a decent layer of fat in your skillet, you are *enhancing its seasoning*!

Steak
As we have already touched base on, for high-quality steak and other similar cuts of meat to really taste heavenly, they need to be cooked on insanely high heat. While cast iron may take what seems like forever to heat up at times, it is so worth the wait.

There are a few popular methods for obtaining a sear that a perfectionist would be proud of. This is the most used method:
1. Heat a pan on high heat or place in oven at 500 degrees.
2. Remove pan *carefully*. Add any room-temperature steak or meat.
3. Let sizzle 30 seconds, flip and sear another 30 seconds.
4. Put skillet back in over 4 to 5 minutes, flipping meat once to achieve the perfect medium-rare steak.
5. If your meat is bone-in, you will need to leave in oven for a tad longer. Use a meat thermometer to ensure it is done.

Pan Pizza
Did someone say PIZZA?! Now I got your attention. If you want to become king or queen of weeknight dinners, all you require is store-bought pizza dough, your favorite toppings, and your handy dandy cast iron skillet. Sound too good to be true? The taste certainly is!
1. Preheat your oven to the highest temperature.
2. Heat skillet over high heat.
3. Stretch dough out and form a flattened round.
4. When pan is smoking hot, add flour to the bottom of it and place dough round on top. *Be careful!* Work with the dough till it forms tightly along the sides. Bring with olive oil.
5. When dough begins to bubble, sprinkle with salt and spread your favorite sauce on all the way to the sides. Top with heaps of your favorite toppings.
6. Bake 10 to 15 minutes and you have a better than The Hut pizza!

Cornbread
You have my permission to slap your grandma for not giving you this cornbread variation! (*Tip: Don't actually slap your granny...that is just cruel.*)

Cornbread is one of the first dishes that comes to mind for most people when they think of cooking with cast iron. Cornbread is amazing and can vary from buttermilk to sweet milk, savory to sweet, and everywhere in-between. There are no wrong answers when it comes to creating a cornbread recipe, but the cast iron skillet will certainly help you get it right the first time!

Pressed sandwiches
You can also leave that pesky and hard to clean sandwich press under your counter too! If you have a hankering for a Cuban Sammie, a panini, or an ooey-gooey grilled cheese, then cast iron is the only way to go to achieve those gorgeous panini marks.

Simply placed your buttered sandwich into preheated cast iron and with another cast iron pan, set on top of sandwich and allow the weight to "press" your sandwich creation!

Bacon
Skip this food suggestion if you are needing to cook a huge batch of crunchy bacon for a crowd, stick with your oven. But if you are looking for just a few pieces of this greasy goodness, then you really need to try it out in cast iron.

The key here is to start off cooking your bacon in a cold skillet. Simply lay out your bacon pieces, set on the stove, and set the heat to medium-high. Be prepared for the bacon to cook much faster than your regular stainless-steel pan. Plus, the cast iron has a magical way of adding an extra dose of crunchiness to your pig!

Hash browns
I don't know about you, but I strongly dislike limp, soggy hash browns. That nice crispy bite of those hash browns at breakfast places are to die for. Now, you don't have to put clothes on or make a trip outside your home! Hash browns made in cast iron are the perfect representation of the baby cast iron, hash browns, and heaven would make if that was possible!

1. Shred potatoes and squeeze excess moisture out.
2. Add a liberal amount of fat to cast iron as it preheats.
3. Spread shredded potatoes into pan. Let cook 5 minutes.
4. Season the uncooked side with pepper, salt, and garlic powder, and whatever else your little heart desires.
5. Fight the temptation to move the hash browns around.
6. Take a peek at cooking side with the help of a spatula. When they reach a gorgeous golden color, flip.
7. Don't leave your pan unattended to cook other side since it will cook faster.

Cookies
If you have a hankering for homemade, ooey-gooey chocolate chip cookies but are too lazy to whip up a whole batch, boy, does the cast iron skillet have a treat for you!

This skillet is the perfect vessel to provide you with an over-sized cookie that can be eaten right out of the pan! All you have to do is adjust your favorite cookie recipes to sit the size of the pan and smooth the dough out. In just 20 minutes, you will have a dessert that could be considered a sin it is so tasty.

S'mores
If that giant skillet cookie wasn't enough to push you into a diabetic coma, then skillet s'mores might be! If it is the wrong season to enjoy an outdoor fire and whip out the graham crackers and marshmallows, then the cast iron skillet has your back. Plus, this version is much better than popping s'more ingredients into the microwave and it is able to keep your s'mores warm for hours.
1. Preheat skillet and melt butter in pan.
2. Add chocolate chips and cover chocolate with a blanket of marshmallows.
3. Bake till marshmallows become just toasted and browned.
4. Use graham crackers as a scoop for this decadent dip!

Dutch babies, crumbles, and cobblers, OH MY!
Say goodbye to a one-track mindset of creating delicious savory dishes with your cast iron. Beyond giant skillet cookies, your grandma's favorite cobbler and crumble recipes can be made to *perfection* with the assistance of your new 'Iron Chef! (Fantastic show by the way, highly recommend binge-watching Iron Chef!)

Just like with your other decadent skillet desserts, cast iron wins above all other kitchen contraptions that merely claim to have the power to create that golden and crunchy crust out mouth craves. If you are looking to be a little healthier, a fun substitution with cast iron desserts is to use coconut oil instead of butter!

And SO MUCH MORE!
If you think I touched all the out-of-the-box goodies that your cast iron skillet can help you create, you are way wrong! Here a few other ideas to try out too!
- Frittatas
- Seared scalloped potatoes
- Herbed potatoes
- Scallops
- And many more! *Be creative* and become your own master chef with the versatility of your cast iron skillet!

What NOT to Cook in Cast Iron

Despite the utter versatility that cast iron allows you to have in your home kitchen, there are a few items that you should stray away from attempting to make in this particular receptacle.

- **Acidic foods** are a *must avoid* when it comes to cast iron. Acid loosens molecules from metal that can get into your food, giving it a nasty metallic taste.

- **Eggs** are another no-no for brand new cast iron pans. With new, not so seasoned skillets, they will just stick and you will clean all the seasoning right from the skillet.

- **Tomato sauce** is highly acidic in nature and can strip your skillet of its seasonings as well as give your food a metal flavor. While you can cook it in short bursts with a splash of wine, avoid simmering these types of sauces for a long period of time.

- **Delicate fishes** that are super flaky can easily fall apart in an extremely hot skillet. The skin will most likely stick to the iron surface, which makes flipping impossible.

- **Cold foods**, unless a recipe specifies to do such, should not be cooked in your cast iron until the skillet has time to properly heat up. If you begin cooking cold food in a pan that is warming up, it will stick.

- **Sticky foods** may cook well in a well-used and seasoned cast iron skillet, but if your skillet is pretty new, these types of eats will likely stick to the surface, making it extremely hard to get clean. And if you do manage to get it clean, you have likely stripped away all that delicious seasoning!

- **Wet food** is another thing that is alright to cook in your cast iron, but be sure to get it out as soon as possible to avoid rusting.

Any Meal...All in ONE Pan!

Whether you are feeling ravishingly hungry or wish to share a meal with an enjoyable person in your life, the cast iron skillet provides you with not only the power to add a variety of ingredients into one pan, but it gives you the freedom to:

- Make meals at a faster pace
- Spend time with loved ones rather than slaving over a stove for hours
- Provides all parties with a plethora of flavors to entice their taste buds

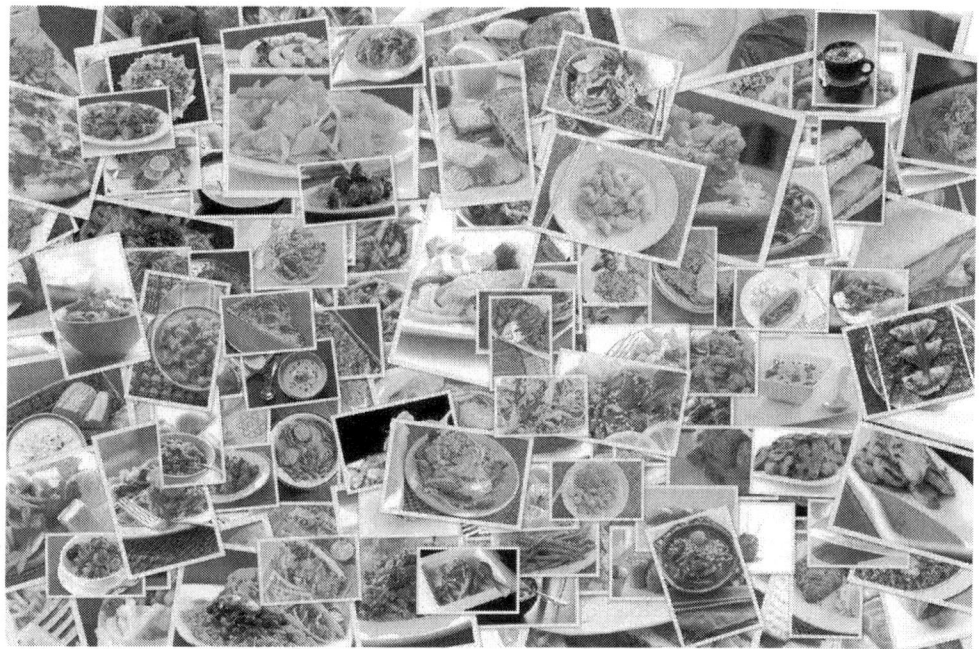

With cast iron, you are not only left with a singular one-pan option for cooking when you don't feel like spending all your free time in the kitchen. The cast iron skillet can literally replace many pieces of cooking equipment and cook foods to acquire a much richer, delicious flavor than say just your grill or stovetop methods. So, don't be afraid to embrace the one-pan recipes!

Better Than Grandma's Cooking

(But don't tell her that!) I have a personal story for your guys to enjoy about my granny's cast iron skillet. Why am I placing this in the middle of the book? Because I really hope you get something out of the story, plus you will get a personal insight as to the power the cast iron skillet has had on my family's cooking.

When my granny passed away at a ripe ole age of 98, it was a daunting task going through all the possessions she had gathered after all that time. The kitchen was the last room to be gone through, and boy did we throw a lot out! One of the items that almost got placed in the 'trash pile' was her tried and true cast iron skillet. I remember her cooking meals in that sucker when I was a tot, which led me to take it home with me.

Let me tell you, discovering and taking granny's skillet for myself was one of the best decisions I ever made. There is no way anyone will ever be able to find a cast iron pan that had all the flavors my granny's lovingly put into this skillet. From being the perfect pan for homemade biscuits to a deep dish for granny's famous apple fritters and everything in-between, I began to realize how underrated these skillets truly were.

While other pots and pans over the years had to be thrown out since they got scratched, bent, broken, and dented, the cast iron pan was still in for the long haul. One evening a family member decided to try out steaks in this skillet, and we were all blown away. They were the best damn skillets we had devoured in *years*. And the plus was that I could taste granny's cooking goodness deep within the steak.

Granny has been gone for 16 years this year and her cast iron skillet is still a prominent cooking vessel in our kitchen. I even have taught my children the basics of using it, which means that if I am not too selfish, I may pass it down to them. Or, better yet, buy them each their own so they too can discover the tasty qualities of a family heirloom passed down through the generations!

Anyways, enough story-telling. Let's get back to the good stuff, shall we?

THE MAGIC IS IN THE SKILLET

If everything you have read so far didn't make you run to your local department store to grab you one of these cast iron miracles, then this chapter will do the trick. (But I do respect your patience and willingness to read this book in one setting!)

The Sizzling Reason Doctors Want You Using Cast Iron

You have learned that you are able to eliminate almost all your other cooking equipment thanks to owning a cast iron skillet. And you have discovered its power in creation a large variety of delicious dishes, but I bet you had no idea the health benefits that cooking with this skillet had!

It is safe to say that the extraordinary benefits of cast iron go far beyond your kitchen. Here are the reasons why cooking with your soon-to-be-favorite piece of culinary equipment does wonders for your physical health!

Retained heat = healthier cooking

While using cast iron is ideal for frying crunchy delights, its ability to retain and maintain heat can help in healthier cooking methods as well. From braising, poaching, and other water-based methods, these types of cooking techniques require little to no oil usage.

Nonstick = excuse to use more often
Since cast iron comes either pre-seasoned or becomes seasoned as you utilize it, it's naturally non-stick, unlike other pans that are now gathering dust in your cupboards. Cast iron is renowned for its ease of cleaning. This alone makes it a better option to use much more often, which allows you to cook healthier meals in a heartbeat with little to no hassle!

Avoid the consumption of unpronounceable chemicals
There will be many times that you may go to grab another non-stick alternative in your kitchen. But keep this section in mind as you do! There are chemicals that are used to help manufacture non-stick pans which can be toxic when exposed to high temperatures. Nobody has time for that, am I right?

One chemical in particular, known as perfluorooctanoic acid (PFOA) is considered to be carcinogenic to us humans. I don't know about you, but that makes me *cringe* thinking about it! (No worries kids, that acid won't be on a spelling test unless you are in school at the World Health Organization.)

Thankfully, PFOA has been phased out of the production process of many pieces of cookware in the United States. In other countries, however, not so much. So, if you have an older non-stick pan in your kitchen, you might want to highly consider trashing it. More room for another cast iron pan!

A boost of iron
If you have heard that cast iron has the power to add a nice dose of extra iron, then I am here to inform you that this is not a myth! Especially for children, women, and vegans who are more prone to having iron deficiencies, the use of cast iron to cook meals could be just the trick to maintain iron levels in the body.

But just *how much* iron gets absorbed into our bodies with cast iron use? This question has been highly debated for years. It is said that foods that take longer to cook, are moist or higher in levels of acidity are known to give cast iron users more iron when consuming the food cooked within.

A.J. Luigi

HOT AS A TWO-DOLLAR PISTOL
(*HEAT DISTRIBUTION*)

As you can imagine, cooking with cast iron sounds pretty simple, and it is. But what many people underestimate are the steps that is takes to ensure safety when handling your new-found favorite culinary tool.

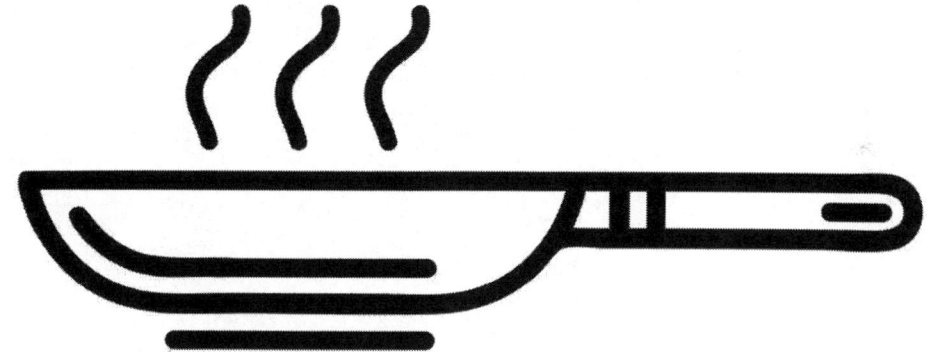

Handle with Care
Stovetop:
Depending on when you purchased your cast iron skillet, you need to be aware of the different handles. If you recently added one of these puppies to your arsenal of kitchen equipment, then you can worry much less, since modern engineering has drastically helped to minimize heat from transferring to the main portion of the skillet to the handle. This minimization keeps your handle cool and perfectly safe to handle without the need of pesky hand mitts.

On the other hand, if you have an older cast iron skillet, knabbed one at a garage sale, or had one passed down to you from your grandparents, then you need to be more careful. Older handles have not been revamped to ensure that the heat from the main portion of the skillet doesn't transfer to the handle. Always use an oven mitt or silicone handle to ensure you don't get badly burned.

Oven:
No matter how masterful your brand-new skillet is, the entirety of *all* cast iron skillets will become a hazard. There is no handle (as far as I know) in the world that will allow you to grip the handle with bare hands when removing from the oven. So, don't think you are superman or woman and do as such! Common sense should be prevalent in all kitchens.

What you *can* do when removing cast iron from your oven is use a thick cloth or oven mitt. Cast iron is also quite heavy, so make sure you can handle taking it out by yourself. If not, gather a stronger troop in the family to help you with this. The last thing you want to do is drop hot cast iron on your foot.

When you set the hot cast iron skillet down, leave the cloth you took it out of the oven with over the handle. This will remind you that the handle is still hot as you dance your way around your kitchen and prepare the other portions of your meal.

A.J. Luigi

CARING FOR YOUR CAST IRON SKILLET

Everyone who owns and utilizes their cast iron skillet and other cast iron culinary tools *love* them. When you love something, you do everything you can to take care of it to ensure its longevity. To keep your cast iron happy and able to provide you with tasty entrees, this chapter is essential!

Easy Cleaning

When it comes to remembering how to clean cast iron, I will ease your mind in informing you that it includes a bigger list of "don'ts" than "do's." There are simple techniques that will ensure your cast iron remains heavenly seasoned, free of rust, and clean.

The tried and true way to clean a cast iron skillet:
What you will need:
- A clean and dry cloth or paper towel
- Stiff brush or sponge
- Vegetable oil or shortening
- Optional: salt
- Stovetop

Cleaning cast iron:
- After use, clean the skillet ASAP, preferably when it is still warm. Don't soak or leave it in the sink to rust.
- Wash the skillet by hand in hot water with your choice of a stiff brush or sponge. DO NOT use steel wool, soap, or place in the dishwasher. These things will strip the seasoning from the pan.
- Scrub off any bits that managed to stick with salt and water. If there is real stubborn residue remaining, pour boiling water into the pan, scrub, and dry.
- Ensure you dry your skillet well over low heat on the stove.
- With a paper towel or clean, dry cloth, place a light coat of melted shortening or vegetable oil. Buff with cloth to remove excess oil.
- Store your clean cast iron skillet in a dry place.

Notes about cast iron cleaning
No, using abrasives like soap or steel wool is not the end of the world when cleaning cast iron, just know that you may have to re-season your pan.

If you have rust to remove:
- Gingerly use steel wool
- Use a hefty sprinkle of salt and rub half a potato over salt
- Re-season pan after removing rust

Restoring Cast Iron

- If the ghost of your granny doesn't come back first to haunt you about the poor state of your rusted cast iron skillet, then I will smack your hand through this book. (SMACK! Feel that? GOOD! What did your cast iron skillet do to you to deserve such bad treatment?!)
- Okay... *deep breath*. I guess rusted cast iron is not impossible to revive, but you should follow the cleaning tips above to avoid having to restore this mess. Thankfully, there are options other than throwing out granny's rusted cast iron!

How to restore a rusty cast iron skillet:
What you will need:
- Foil
- Cooking oil of choice (I recommend vegetable oil)
- Dish towel or paper towels
- Dish soap
- Sponge, scouring pad, or other type of scrub brush
- Steel wool
- Oven

How to restore cast iron:
- With fine steel wool, remove rust from pan. Scour till the area is once again returned to its raw cast iron state.
- Thoroughly wash the skillet in mild dish soap and warm water. Use a bristle brush to scrub with.
- Right after cleaning, thoroughly dry your skillet with a dish towel.
- Pour a small amount of your choice of cooking oil into skillet and ensure the oil covers the entire portion of the inside of pan.
- When you are oiling skillet, do not forget to spread oil over the bottom of skillet as well as the handle.
- Preheat your oven to 350 degrees and place your cast iron skillet in the oven for 60 minutes.
- Ensure your skillet is completely dry before turning off the heat and allowing the skillet to cool. YAY! RESTORED!

Cast Iron Skillet Sins

As mentioned in the first chapter of this book, any utensils that are made from the wonders of cast iron can easily endure centuries of use and abuse when taken care of properly. There are quite a few sins that will inhibit the longevity of your cast iron skillet that you should do your best to avoid at all costs!

- **Putting off using it** will keep your pan from gathering the fats and oils it needs to become conditioned to last longer.
- While seasoning is the bomb, **over seasoning your skillet can cause much more harm than good**. You cannot rush the seasoning process! If you apply more than just a slight layer of oil when you cook, you will turn out with a goopy layer of nastiness rather than the shiny black finish.

- **Failure to preheat** your skillet will give you uneven cooking spots as well as hot spots that will scorch your meals. Preheat cast iron for at least 5 to 10 minutes over medium heat before adding anything to it. To test the heat, flick water into it. When sizzling, it is ready!
- When you are new to cast iron cooking, you cannot **have the mindset that a new pan will be as non-stick** as a Teflon pan, for instance. When experimenting, make sure to add a bit of fat to get the non-stick surface you need.
- **Using metal spatulas** with cast iron is a big no-no, especially the ones equipped with a straight front edge. I am cringing over here thinking about your poor cast iron! The metal from these utensils will remove the polish from the pan, making it more and more non-stick and harder to use as time goes on.
- **Using soap** and water to clean your cast iron should be done only on a rare basis, if *ever*. Lean towards rinsing out your pan after cooking in hot water and drying, rather than exposing it to the abrasiveness of soap.
- Unlike your other kitchen equipment, never **soak** your cast iron in the sink. Bring water to a simmer on the stove and use a brush to remove bits.
- **Putting your cast iron away wet** is just as bad as putting up a horse when wet! Wet iron naturally rusts and will totally ruin your years of hard work in seasoning the pan.
- **Placing a super-hot cast iron skillet into ice cold water** can possible make the iron crack, which is one of the worst things you can do! Allow your skillet to come back to room temperature, always.
- If you store your cast iron in the oven, make sure you take it out before preheating your oven. This will save you the time to take the host pan from the oven and it will also save your seasoning from being eliminated.

PRO TIPS FROM THE CHEF!

I don't like to label myself as a cast iron extraordinaire but for the sake of this book, I will take that namesake happily. I absolutely love my cast iron skillet and it has changed the way that I cook delicious and healthy meals for myself and my family. Now that you have learned some cool aspects about this skillet, what you can create and how to take care of your new investment, this chapter will cover some essential tips of being a cast iron owner.

The Pro Way to Season Your Cast Iron

If you are a total newbie to the world of cast iron, you have probably been wondering how to master this whole 'seasoning' business. I know I was confused about it after I was gifted my first cast iron skillet.

What *is* Seasoning?

Seasoning is the oil that is baked onto the pan. It helps to prevent rust from developing and it provides chefs with an easy-release finish that improves more with use and time. Seasoning refers to the initial finish this piece of cookware has, as well as the continuing process of maintaining that special finish.

About the Oil(s)

The *oil* that is often used for pre-seasoned pans is made of proteins that have soy-related aspects removed. This oil does not include paints, peanut oils or animal fats. Various brands of cast iron cookware will have slight variations of seasoning finishes. This variation doesn't affect the overall performance of the pan.

All kinds of fats and oil can be utilized to season cast iron cookware, depending on how available it is, it's price, and the overall effectiveness it has on cast iron. It is often recommended to use vegetable oil or melted shortening or canola oil spray. Back in the good old days, lard was used to season cast iron and is still used as a seasoning method today. But, it is not highly recommended unless you plan to use your cast iron skillet on a regular basis.

I cannot stress enough the importance of adding a thin layer of fat or oil after each and every cleaning of your cast iron. This helps to ensure its longevity!

Tricks to Even Better Cast Iron Seasoning

- Seasoning too sticky? This is a red flag of excess oil buildup. Put cast iron into oven at 400 degrees for an hour. Let cool.
- If you notice a dark residue in your pan after cooking acidic foods or meals that require extreme heat, don't panic. This is just your seasoning hard at work and it will go away with use and proper care.
- Notice a small bubble at the tip of one of both handles that chips away and creates a brownish color? This is not rust. It is the result of your cookware being seasoned during manufacturing. This will disappear with use and proper care.

Cast Iron Pro Cooking Tips

If you have just purchased or restored a cast iron skillet, then the first thing you should cook is bacon! No complaints here! It creates a delicious array of flavors to become absorbed into your new or restored cast iron seasoning.

To master the perfect steak in cast iron:
- Preheat pan till very hot.
- Season both sides of steak with salt and pepper.
- Add a teaspoon of coconut oil into pan.
- Add seasoned steak to pan and sear first side.
- Touch meat lightly to press into pan and ensure evenness.
- Allow to seat 3 to 4 minutes.
- Flip steak and allow the other side to sear 3 to 4 minutes.
- Then sear sides of steak 1 to 3 minutes.
- Use a meat thermometer to ensure doneness of steak, anything at 120 degrees and above.
- Allow meat to rest at least 7 minutes before slicing.
- DEVOUR!

Note: Don't be too afraid or hesitant at trying new ingredients in your cast iron skillet, even ones that you have previously not enjoyed. The seasoning of this skillet allows richer and broadened flavors to jump out to your taste buds and allows you to open your eyes to what seemingly bland ingredients can really do!

Conclusion

We do have to admit that the Lodge cast iron skillets that we used for our recipes are pretty awesome, right? If you don't think so, your opinion does not matter here. These skillets have the power to cook entire meals without the hassle of multiple pans, has an unknowing positive touch on your physical health, and can be used in a variety of cooking methods. How many other kitchen gadgets can do that?

I hope that you found this book valuable and packed with the information you needed to go out and purchase yourself a cast iron skillet. Even if you don't use it often, you can rest assured that you have a weapon you don't have to aim. Just batta batta SWING! (Kidding, only do this when your life is in danger, even if it is tempting to shut the in-laws up during the holidays.)

Now it is your turn to take this information and start impressing friends and family with tasty meals that satisfy.

Cooking with the Lodge Cast Iron Skillet Cookbook

YOURS FOR LOOKING

"BONUS" Get Your Marinades for Meats & Veggies!

Get your very own Air Fryer Marinade Quick Start Guide! This quick start guide will show you how to get the best tasting foods when cooking from your air fryer! **GET YOURS NOW** by just simply clicking the button below! **Enjoy!**

http://eepurl.com/dzsApr

A.J. Luigi

BEST BEEF:

Cast Iron Oven Baked Beef Stew

This comfort food dish cooks inside the oven and not on the stove. The difference will please your taste buds.

Prep Time: 15 minutes
Cook Time: 5 hours
Makes: 8 Servings

INGREDIENTS:
2 ½ lbs. beef stew meat chunks
8 carrots, chopped
3 medium white onions, quartered
5 medium white potatoes, quartered
2 cans Sweet Peas
2 bay leaves
2 beef bouillon cubes
1 tbsp. sugar
1 tbsp. salt
¼ tbsp. thyme
1 tbsp. black pepper
¼ cup cornstarch
1 28-oz. can whole tomatoes
1 cup water

DIRECTIONS:
- Set the oven temperature at 300 degrees.
- Pour all the ingredients in the Lodge Cast Iron Skillet.
- Cover and cook for 5 hours, stir once or twice
- Serve immediately and enjoy.

Cast Iron Skillet Nachos

Skillet made nachos is a great dish to make on those busy nights, or even on game day. No matter the occasion they will be a hit in your household.

Prep Time: 5 minutes
Cook Time: 26 minutes
Makes: 8 Servings

INGREDIENTS:

2 tbsp. vegetable oil
1 red onion, chopped
1 lb. lean ground beef
1 ¼ tbsp. chili powder
1 garlic clove, minced
¼ tsp. dried oregano
½ tsp. ground cumin
½ tsp. ground coriander
¼ tsp. cayenne pepper
1/8 tsp. salt

½ cup chicken broth
4 cups Mexican blend shredded cheese
2 cups tortilla chips
¼ cup jalapenos, chopped
2 green onions, sliced
Salsa, to taste
Guacamole, to taste
Sour cream, to taste

DIRECTIONS:

- Set the oven temperature at 400 degrees.
- Pour the vegetable oil in the pan and heat on the stove for 3 minutes
- Add the onion and cook for 5 minutes.
- Next, add the ground beef and cook for another 5 minutes, until brown.
- Then stir in the salt, garlic, chili powder, cumin, coriander, and cayenne and let cook for 1 more minute.
- Stir in the brown and cook for 2 minutes until evaporated.
- Transfer the ground beef mixture in a bowl with the cheese.
- Clean the skillet with a paper towel and then spread out half of the tortilla chips in the skillet and sprinkle half the cheese, ground beef mixture, and jalapenos. Repeat the process.
- Place the skillet in the oven and bake for 15 minutes
- Sprinkle with green onions, and top with salsa, sour cream and guacamole.
- Serve immediately and enjoy.

Montana Style Cowboy Skillet Steak

This will be one of the best steaks you have ever had. The skillet helps give the steak an extra char that you wouldn't get on the mere grill alone.

Prep Time: 20 minutes
Cook Time: 60 minutes
Makes: 4 Servings

INGREDIENTS:
1 2 lb. porterhouse steak
¼ tsp. salt
¼ tsp. pepper
1 tbsp. vegetable oil
2 tablespoons butter
3 garlic cloves, minced
Fresh thyme, to taste
Fresh rosemary, to taste
Fresh oregano, to taste

DIRECTIONS:
- Set the grill temperature t0 400 degrees.
- Heat the covered skillet on the grill for 15 minutes.
- Season the steak with salt and pepper
- Coat the skillet with oil and use tongs to place the steak in the skillet for 10 minutes until dark brown.
- Turn the steak over on the fatty side and hold upright with the tongs. Cook for 2 more minutes.
- Turn over onto the uncooked side and place lid on top. Grill for 10 minutes.
- Next, add the butter, garlic and herbs to the skillet and cook for 3 minutes.
- Spoon the mixture over the steak until it is covered in it.
- Transfer the steak to a plate and let the steak breathe for 10 minutes.
- Serve immediately and enjoy.

Broccoli Beef

Your favorite Chinese food dish made in your own kitchen. Now, everyone will be asking you to cook when they want Chinese.

Prep Time: 5 minutes
Cook Time: 40 minutes
Makes: 2 Servings

INGREDIENTS:

¾ lb. steak
¼ cup soy sauce
2 tbsp. soy sauce
½ tsp. baking soda
1 large broccoli head, cut in florets
1 tsp. cornstarch
1 tsp. ginger, chopped

1 tsp. garlic, chopped
2 tsp. sesame oil
2 tbsp. brown sugar
1 ½ tsp. vegetable oil
Green onions, to taste
Sesame seeds, to taste

DIRECTIONS:
- Prepare the steaks by cutting into strips.
- Marinate with the ¼ cup soy sauce and baking soda for 15 minutes to an hour.
- Preheat the skillet over medium heat on the stove.
- Mix together the soy sauce, cornstarch, garlic, ginger, sugar and sesame oil.
- Drain the steak and dry with paper towels.
- Add 1/3 cup water to the skillet and turn the heat to high. Pour in the broccoli and steam until all the water has evaporated. Drain the broccoli and set aside.
- Pour vegetable oil to the pan and add the steak. Cook for 2 minutes. Toss so it is evenly cooked then remove.
- Add the sauce to the skillet and boil. Toss the steak in and stir until the steak is combined thoroughly.
- Do the same with the broccoli.
- Serve immediately with the green onions and sesame seed. Pour over rice and enjoy.

Ground Beef Shepard's Pie

The ground beef in this dish makes it easier to cook &and adds a lot of flavor!

Prep Time: 15 minutes
Cook Time: 60 minutes
Makes: 4 Servings

INGREDIENTS:
1 lb. ground beef
¾ tsp. dried oregano
1 tsp. salt
1 tsp. pepper
4 tbsp. tomato paste
½ cup beef broth
1 tsp. Worcestershire sauce
6 oz. carrots, shredded
8 oz. mushrooms, chopped
2 garlic cloves, minced
1 cup peas
1 cup corn
4 cups mashed potatoes
1 cup cheddar cheese, shredded

DIRECTIONS:
- Set the oven temperature at 375 degrees.
- Cook the beef in the skillet over medium heat.
- Strain the meat of grease and out back in the skillet.
- Season with oregano, salt and pepper.
- Stir in the tomato paste, broth, Worcestershire sauce, carrots, mushrooms, and garlic. Cook for 10 minutes. Then add the peas and corn. Cook for 1 more minute.
- Warm the mashed potatoes in the microwave.
- Pour half of the cheese on top of the meat mixture and then spread the potatoes evenly on top.
- Sprinkle the rest of the cheese on top and bake for 40 minutes.
- Serve immediately and enjoy.

Cheesy Skillet Hamburgers

These cheesy skillet hamburgers are a great recipe to make any time of the year. And with less mess to clean up.

Prep Time: 5 minutes
Cook Time: 11 minutes
Makes: 4 Servings

INGREDIENTS:

2 lbs. ground beef
2 tbsp. vegetable oil
4 tbsp. water
8 slices cheddar cheese
4 hamburger buns

Toppings:
Lettuce
Tomatoes
Mayo
Mustard
Ketchup
Pickles

DIRECTIONS:

- Divide the ground beef into 4 hamburger patties.
- Set the skillet on the stove and heat the vegetable oil over medium heat.
- Cook the burgers for 2 minutes on each side.
- Pour the water in the pan, cover the burgers and cook for 1 more minute.
- Take off the lid. Place 2 slices of cheese on each burger and cook for 1 more minute.
- Place each burger on a bottom bun, top with toppings and finish with the top bun.
- Serve immediately and enjoy.

Beefy, Cheesy Skillet Lasagna

Lasagna on the stove? This recipe will change how you look at lasagna forever.

Prep Time: 5 minutes
Cook Time: 40 minutes
Makes: 6 Servings

INGREDIENTS:

1 28 oz. can of crushed tomatoes
1 can roasted garlic tomato sauce
¼ cup water
1 tbsp. olive oil
1 medium red onion, diced
4 garlic cloves, minced
¼ tsp. salt
¼ tsp. pepper
¼ tsp. crushed red pepper
¾ lb. ground beef
¼ lb. Italian sausage
8 lasagna noodles, broken into sections
½ cup of ricotta cheese
4 oz. mozzarella, sliced thin and then torn into pieces
Shaved Parmesan, for taste

DIRECTIONS:

- Start by mixing the crushed tomatoes, tomato sauce and water in a bowl.
- Heat the olive oil in the cast iron skillet.
- Add the onion into the skillet and cook until soft. Pour in the garlic, salt, pepper, and red pepper flakes and cook for 2 minutes.
- Now, add the meat and cook until full brown for about 10 minutes.
- Layer the noodles on top of the meat mixture and pour the tomato sauce over the top.
- Boil the mixture and then reduce to a medium low temperature.
- After it boils, stir the noodles into the meat and then drop spoonful of the ricotta into the mixture.
- Stir the mixture.
- Next, place the mozzarella on top, cover and cook for 5 minutes.
- Serve immediately with basil and Parmesan and enjoy.

PULSATING POULTRY:

Comfort Skillet Chicken Pot Pie

This one skillet chicken pot pie will be a go to on those cold and rainy nights when your bones are craving comfort food.

Prep Time: 20 minutes
Cook Time: 50 minutes
Makes: 6 Servings

INGREDIENTS:

4 chicken breasts
5 tbsp. butter
¼ white onion, diced
5 tbsp. all-purpose flour
1 ½ cups chicken broth
1 cup milk

3 cups mixed carrots and peas
½ cup celery, sliced
½ tsp. celery seed
9 inch pie crust
Salt, to taste
Pepper, to taste

DIRECTIONS:

- Add chicken to a pot of water, and bring to a boil.
- Reduce the heat to medium and cook for 18 minutes. Skim the foam when needed.
- In another pan, melt the butter and add the onions. Cook for 2 minutes until soft.
- Pour in the flour and whisk together for 2 minutes.
- Slowly add the broth, and milk and continue to whisk. Cook for 15 minutes until it thickens.
- Now add the peas, carrots, celery, celery seed, salt and pepper together.
- Remove the chicken from the pot, drain and chop into cubes.
- Place the chicken in the skillet and pour the sauce over the top.
- Roll the pie crust on top and tuck in the edges. Take a knife and make slits all around.
- Put the skillet on a baking sheet to catch the drips.
- Set the oven on 425 degrees and bake for 35 minutes.
- Let it cool for 10 minutes.
- Serve immediately and enjoy.

Sweet Potato and Savory Ground Turkey Skillet

This is not your average turkey and sweet potato dish. This dish will definitely change how you feel about turkey and sweet potato.

Prep Time: 10 minutes
Cook Time: 17 minutes
Makes: 4 Servings

INGREDIENTS:
2 tbsp. olive oil
1 lb. ground turkey
1 tsp. garlic clove, minced
½ cup white onion, diced
½ cup yellow pepper, diced
1 ½ cup sweet potato, diced
½ cup mozzarella cheese, shredded
Salt, to taste
Pepper to taste,
Red chili flakes, to taste
Fresh parsley, garnish

DIRECTIONS:
- Heat the olive oil in the skillet.
- Add in the ground turkey and garlic. Cook the turkey for 7 minutes.
- Pour in the onions and yellow peppers until the onions are soft.
- Next, add in the sweet potato, salt, pepper and chili pepper.
- Place the lid on the skillet and cook until the mixture is tender.
- Set the oven to 400 degrees.
- Add the cheese and put the skillet in the oven and cook for 5 minutes.
- When done, remove from the oven and sprinkle with parsley.
- Serve immediately and enjoy.

Chicken Sausage with Basil and Gnocchi

Chicken sausage pairs great with these tomatoes in this dish. The sweetness of the apple in the sausage gives this Italian dish a little unintended added flavor

Prep Time: 15 minutes
Cook Time: 10 minutes
Makes: 4 Servings

INGREDIENTS:
1 lb. gnocchi
3 links chicken apple sausage, cooked and cut into coins
1 pint grape tomatoes, sliced in half
2 oz. fresh basil, cut into strips
Salt, to taste
Pepper, to taste

DIRECTIONS:
- Bring a pot of salt water to boil.
- Pour in the gnocchi and cook for 2 minutes.
- Drain the gnocchi and sprinkle with olive oil.
- Pour some olive oil in the skillet and heat.
- Add the sausage and cook for 3 minutes.
- Push the sausage to the side of the skillet and add the tomatoes, skin down.
- Cook the tomatoes for 2 minutes, and stir with the sausage. Cook for 2 more minutes.
- Stir in the gnocchi and combine. Make sure the tomatoes to not become sauce.
- Remove from the heat and stir in the basil. Season with salt and pepper.
- Serve immediately and enjoy.

Skillet Roasted Chicken

This succulent rosemary roasted chicken is one of the best ways to cook chicken.

Prep Time: 40 minutes
Cook Time: 90 minutes
Makes: 4 Servings

INGREDIENTS:

1 whole 3 lb. chicken
3 tbsp. butter
1 garlic clove, minced
1 ¼ tsp. fresh rosemary, minced
½ tsp. salt
1 tsp. pepper
1 white onion, cut into chunks
2 red potatoes, cut into chunks

2 sweet potatoes, cut into chunks
2 garlic cloves, sliced
2 tbsp. olive oil
1 tsp. herbs de Provence
¼ cup white wine
1 tsp. Dijon mustard
½ cup chicken broth

DIRECTIONS:

- Set the oven to 350.
- In a pan, melt the butter, garlic, salt, pepper and rosemary. Set aside.
- Loosen the breast meat and the skin to form a pocket in the chicken.
- Spoon in some of the butter mixture into the skin and massage it evenly.
- Place ½ tbsp. of the butter mixture and brush it on top of the chicken.
- Place the chicken in the skillet and tie the legs together.
- Place the onions and potatoes around the chicken and sprinkle with the olive oil, salt, pepper, and herbs.
- Put the skillet in the oven and cook for 90 minutes. Baste the chicken with its juices every 20 minutes.
- Remove the chicken from the oven and set on a cutting board.
- Let rest for 10 minutes.
- Deglaze the pan with the wine and heat until it has reduced about 1/3 percent. Add in the mustard and whisk in the chick broth until the sauce has reached the consistency you desire.
- Carve the chicken and spoon the sauce over the chicken and vegetables.
- Serve immediately and enjoy.

Skillet Tangy Lemon Turkey

We don't often think past stuffing, and cranberry sauce when we think of turkey. This lemon tangy turkey breast will show you that there are other things you can do to turkey besides smother it in gravy.

Prep Time: 4 minutes
Cook Time: 6 minutes
Makes: 2 Servings

INGREDIENTS:
4 turkey breasts, thinly sliced
1 tbsp. canola oil
1 tbsp. fresh mixed herbs, chopped
1 cup chicken broth
4 cups spinach
Lemon wedges
Salt, to taste
Pepper, to taste

DIRECTIONS:
- Heat the cast iron skillet over medium high heat
- Sprinkle the salt and pepper over the turkey breasts.
- Pour the canola oil in the skillet and place in the breasts in the skillet.
- Cook for 2 minutes.
- Turn the breasts over and drizzle with the herbs.
- Cook for 2 more minutes.
- Remove and set aside.
- Pour the broth and the spinach in the skillet and steam the spinach for about 2 minutes.
- Remove the greens with tongs and divide between the two plates.
- Next, reduce the by broth by half, squeeze the lemon juice and then pour over the turkey breasts.
- Serve immediately and enjoy.

Prosciutto Wrapped Skillet Seared Chicken

Thin sliced Italian ham pairs great with the chicken. Add the pesto sauce and this is a chicken you don't want to miss.

Prep Time: 20 minutes
Cook Time: 50 minutes
Makes: 4 Servings

INGREDIENTS:
3 chicken breasts, thinly sliced
3 tbsp. flour
4 slices prosciutto
2 tbsp. olive oil
1 bunch asparagus
¼ cup basil pesto
1/3 cup cream
Salt, to taste
Pepper, to taste

DIRECTIONS:
- Lightly season the chicken with salt and pepper.
- Submerge the chicken in the flour and then wrap in a piece of prosciutto
- Heat the olive oil in the cast iron skillet.
- Add the chicken and cook for 6 minutes.
- Flip and cook for 5 minutes.
- In a small pot, add 3 inches of water, cover and let boil.
- Wash and snap the ends off of the asparagus.
- Cut the asparagus into pieces. Steam for 5 minutes.
- Rinse with cold water and set aside.
- In a separate bowl, combine the pesto and cream. Pour the mixture over the chicken, and the asparagus.
- Boil the mixture together.
- Turn off the heat when done.
- Serve immediately and enjoy.

Cooking with the Lodge Cast Iron Skillet Cookbook

FANTASTIC FISH:

Buttery Tarragon Encrusted Seared Salmon

Salmon and butter are not two ingredients you hear often. But, in this recipe you will see how the butter compliments this fish,

Prep Time: 5 minutes
Cook Time: 13 minutes
Makes: 2 Servings

INGREDIENTS:

16 oz. salmon cut in two pieces
¼ tsp. salt
¼ tsp. pepper
1 cup cherry tomatoes, halved
2 tbsp. fresh tarragon, chopped
1 tbsp. butter, unsalted

DIRECTIONS:
- Set the oven to 450 degrees.
- Spray the salmon with avocado or olive oil spray.
- Sprinkle salt and pepper over the salmon.
- Place the skillet on the stove and heat on high for 1 minute.
- Spray the pan with the oil.
- Next, place the salmon in the pan, skin side up and cook for 1 minute.
- With a non-metal spatula, turn the salmon over and sear for 1 more minute.
- Place the tomatoes around the fish and season with the tarragon.
- Add the butter by placing two pieces on separate sides of the pan.
- Put the pan in the oven and cook for 10 minutes.
- Remove from the oven and garnish with the rest of the tarragon.
- Serve immediately and enjoy.

Zesty Shrimp and Crab Bake

Crab and shrimp are the two cousins of the seafood world. This creaminess of this casserole will make you add this recipe to your comfort food list.

Prep Time: 10 minutes
Cook Time: 15 minutes
Makes: 4 Servings

INGREDIENTS:

1 cup lump crabmeat
12 oz. raw shrimp, peeled and deveined
2 celery ribs, diced
1 medium white onion, diced
1 medium green bell pepper, stem, seed and dice
2 garlic cloves, minced
2 tbsp. butter, unsalted

2 tsp. flour
1 cup shrimp stock
3 tbsp. heavy cream
1 bunch green onions, chopped
½ cup fresh bread crumbs
½ lime juice
Ground cayenne pepper, to taste
Chili powder, to taste

DIRECTIONS:

- Heat the skillet over medium heat and melt the butter.
- Toss in the celery, onion, garlic, and bell pepper.
- Cook for 5 minutes. Stir until the vegetables are soft.
- Sprinkle the cayenne pepper and chili powder over the mixture. Add the flour and cook for 1 minute.
- Pour in the fish stock and increase the heat and boil.
- Cook for 5 minutes, until it has thickened into sauce.
- Reduce the heat to medium low and add the crabmeat and shrimp to the skillet with the heavy cream.
- Stir and cook for 2 minutes.
- Combine the bread crumbs with the green onions and scatter over the top of the skillet.
- Transfer the skillet to the oven.
- Broil for 1 minute.
- Squeeze the lime juice.
- Serve immediately and enjoy.

Korean Tuna Cakes

This exotic dish teaches us another way to make tuna minus the mayo. Complete with dipping sauce it becomes a fun dish you can make for your kids as a snack.

Prep Time: 10 minutes
Cook Time: 7 minutes
Makes: 4 Servings

INGREDIENTS:

1 6.5 oz. can tuna, drained
1 egg, beaten
2 sprigs green onion, chopped
¼ red onion, chopped
1 red cayenne chili pepper
1 green cayenne chili pepper

1 tsp. all-purpose flour
1/8 tsp. salt
1/8 tsp. pepper
½ cup panko
Olive oil, for cooking

Dipping Sauce
1 tbsp. soy sauce
1 tbsp. water
1 tbsp. rice vinegar
2 tsp. white sugar

DIRECTIONS:

- Mix all the ingredients together, except the olive oil and the panko.
- Divide into four sections to make for round medium tuna cakes.
- Smother the cakes in the panko.
- Heat the olive oil in the skillet over medium heat.
- Put the cakes in the skillet and cook each side for 6 minutes until browned
- Cover the skillet and cook for 3 more minutes until the inside is cooked.
- Remove from the stove.
- Mix all of the dipping sauce ingredients together.
- Serve immediately with the dipping sauce and enjoy.

Creole Style Grouper

Cajun style grouper is one of those recipes that you can pair along with some dirty rice or jambalaya. Whatever the case, the seasonings in this dish speak for themselves.

Prep Time: 5 minutes
Cook Time: 15 minutes
Makes: 4 Servings

INGREDIENTS:

1 lb. grouper
3 tbsp. olive oil
4 cloves garlic, minced
3 tbsp. special seasoning
2 tbsp. Parmesan cheese, grated

Special Seasoning:
2 ½ tbsp. paprika
2 tbsp. salt
2 tbsp. garlic powder
1 ¼ tbsp. black pepper
1 tbsp. onion powder
1 tbsp. cayenne pepper
1 ¼ tbsp. dried oregano
1 ¼ tbsp. dried thyme

DIRECTIONS:
- Combine all of the special seasoning in a bowl and set aside.
- Se the oven to 435 degrees.
- Put the skillet in the oven to preheat.
- In a separate bowl, combine the oil, garlic, special seasoning, and parmesan cheese.
- Brush the fish with the mixture and place in the skillet.
- Bake for 15 minutes until fish is flaky.
- Serve immediately and enjoy.

Spanish Skillet Tilapia

The great thing about tilapia is that you can do anything to it and it will still taste good. In this recipe, we combined it with tomatoes, olives and jalapenos for a little kick.

Prep Time: 10 minutes
Cook Time: 10 minutes
Makes: 4 Servings

INGREDIENTS:

4 tilapia fillets
3 tbsp. olive oil
2 tomatoes, chopped
1 red bell pepper, sliced
1 medium red onion, sliced
1/3 cup garlic tomato sauce
3 garlic cloves, minced
1/3 cup olives, pitted and halved
1 ½ tbsp. capers, rinsed and drained
1 tbsp. jalapeno peppers, chopped
¼ cup chicken stock
1 ¼ oregano
Salt, to taste
Pepper, to taste

DIRECTIONS:

- Heat the oil in the skillet.
- Pour in the chopped tomatoes, sliced bell peppers, and onion.
- Season with salt and stir.
- Reduce the heat to medium, cover with the lid and cook for 4 minutes.
- Next, add the minced garlic, olives, capers, jalapeno peppers, chicken stock and tomato sauce.
- Season the vegetables again with oregano, pepper and salt, and stir.
- Sprinkle the filets with salt and pepper.
- Place on top of the sauce and toss over the top of the fish.
- Cover the fish and cook for 6 minutes.
- Remove from the stove.
- Serve immediately and enjoy.

Herb Blackened Trout

A classic dish made easy. In 30 minutes, you will have a dish that everyone will be begging to try again and again.

Prep Time: 20 minutes
Cook Time: 10 minutes
Makes: 4 Servings

INGREDIENTS:
6 trout fillets
1 ¼ tbsp. paprika
2 tsp. dry mustard
1 tsp. cayenne pepper
1 tsp. ground cumin
1 tsp. white pepper
1 tsp. black pepper
1 tsp. dried thyme
1 tsp. salt
¾ cup unsalted butter, melted
¼ cup unsalted butter, melted

DIRECTIONS:
- Combine the paprika, dry mustard, cayenne pepper, cumin, black pepper, white pepper, thyme and salt into a small bowl. Set aside.
- Heat the skillet on high heat.
- In a shallow bowl, pour the ¾ cup butter. Dip the fillets in the butter.
- Sprinkle with the spice mixture on both sides.
- Set the fillets into the pan, leaving room.
- Pour 1 tsp. butter over each fillet.
- Cook for 2 minutes or until the fish has a charred look.
- Turn the fish over and repeat the process.
- Remove from the heat.
- Serve immediately and enjoy.

A.J. Luigi

PERFECTED PORK:

One Skillet Pork Cacciatore

This pork chop laid on top of noodles and vegetables gives an Italian feel with something different. After you've tasted it you will wonder why you chicken used to be the star of this dish. Someone was sadly misinformed.

Prep Time: 30 minutes
Cook Time: 30 minutes
Makes: 4 Servings

INGREDIENTS:

- 4 bon- in pork chops
- 1 ½ tsp. salt
- 1 ½ tsp. pepper
- 2 tbsp. butter, unsalted
- 8 oz. cremini mushrooms, sliced
- 1 cup red onion, chopped
- 1 cup green bell pepper, chopped
- ¼ cup carrot, chopped
- 2 tbsp. tomato paste
- 1 tsp. garlic, chopped
- ¼ cup dry white wine
- 1 can whole peeled tomatoes
- ½ cup chicken stock
- 1 rosemary sprig
- 1 bay leaf
- ½ cup olives, pitted and halved
- 6 cup Bucatini pasta, cooked
- 2 tbsp. fresh parsley, chopped

DIRECTIONS:

- Set the oven to 400 degrees and season the pork chops with 1 tsp. of salt and ¾ tsp. pepper then heat the butter over high heat in the skillet.
- Place the pork chops in the skillet and cook for 3 minutes on each side.
- Take out of skillet and transfer the pork chops to a rimmed baking sheet.
- Place in the oven and cook for 10-15 minutes. (check for doneness)
- Remove and let rest for 10 minutes.
- While the pork is cooking in the oven, add the mushrooms, onion, bell pepper, and carrot to the skillet. Spread evenly and cook for 2 minutes.
- Stir and cook for 2 more minutes. Then add tomato paste, garlic and remaining salt and pepper. Cook for 1 minute, stirring constantly.
- Add the wine and simmer down by half for 30 seconds, then add the tomatoes, and smash with a wooden spoon.
- Pour in the rosemary, chicken stock, and bay leaf, and bring to a boil.
- Reduce the heat to medium and add the olives and cool for 15 minutes.
- Place the pork and sauce over the pasta and serve immediately and enjoy.

Cast Iron Skillet Fried Ham Steak

Pan fry this steak without the oil. The butter and brown sugar will give the sweetness that will have this ham melt in your mouth.

Prep Time: 10 minutes
Cook Time: 15minutes
Makes: 2 Servings

INGREDIENTS:
1 8 oz. bone-in ham steak, fully cooked
5 tbsp. butter, cubed
5 tbsp. brown sugar

DIRECTIONS:
- Heat the skillet over medium heat.
- Place the ham steak in the skillet and cook for 4 minutes per side, until browned.
- Remove the ham and drain.
- Melt the butter in the skillet.
- Add the brown sugar.
- Return the ham to the skillet and cook over medium-low heat for 10 minutes.
- Remove from the heat.
- Serve immediately and enjoy.

Pork Tenderloin with Vegetable Medley

Pork tenderloin paired with various vegetables is a one-cast iron skillet meal in itself.

Prep Time: 10 minutes
Cook Time: 30 minutes
Makes: 4 Servings

INGREDIENTS:

1 2 ½ lb. boneless pork loin
2 tbsp. canola oil
2 tbsp. butter, unsalted
1 shallot, minced
2 garlic cloves, minced
2 cups squash, diced
2 cups zucchini, diced

1 cup tomatoes, diced
1 tsp. basil
1 tsp. parsley
1 tsp. thyme
Salt, to taste
Pepper, to taste

DIRECTIONS:
- Set the oven to 375 degrees.
- Sprinkle both sides of the pork with salt and pepper.
- Preheat the skillet on the stove.
- Warm up the oil and then add the pork loin.
- Sear on both sides.
- Transfer the skillet to the oven and cook for 25 minutes.
- Remove from the oven and set the meat on a cutting board.
- Return the skillet to the stove and place on medium heat.
- Melt the butter and scrape all of the brown bits off of the skillet.
- When the butter is foaming, add the shallot and garlic until it is wilted. About 2 minutes.
- Next, add the squash and the zucchini and cook for 6 minutes. Stir.
- Then add the tomatoes and herbs, and stir to wilt the tomatoes and the herbs.
- Spoon the Vegetable medley onto plates and top with pork slices.
- Serve immediately and enjoy.

Sizzling Spicy New Mexico Ham Steak

Forget the butter and honey. Let's make this steak sizzle.

Prep Time: 5 minutes
Cook Time: 15 minutes
Makes: 4 Servings

INGREDIENTS:
1 ½ lb. ham steak
2 tsp. chili powder
1 ¼ tsp. dried oregano
¼ tsp. ground cayenne pepper
¼ tsp. fresh ground black pepper
1 tsp. brown sugar
1 tsp. unsalted butter, melted

DIRECTIONS:
- Heat the iron skillet over medium high heat.
- In a small bowl, mix the chili powder, cayenne, black peppers, brown sugar, butter and the dried oregano together.
- Rub mixture all over the steaks.
- Put the ham in the pan and cook for 6 minutes until black in various places.
- Turn and cook on the other side for 4 minutes.
- Remove from the stove and let the meat rest for 5 minutes.
- Serve immediately and enjoy.

Bacon Wrapped Pork

Bacon makes everything taste better, even its cousin, pork.

Prep Time: 10 minutes
Cook Time: 30 minutes
Makes: 4 Servings

INGREDIENTS:
8 slices bacon
2 lbs. pork tenderloin
1 tbsp. garlic powder
1 ¼ seasoned salt
1 ½ tsp. dried basil
1 ½ tsp. dried oregano
3 tbsp. butter
2 tbsp. olive oil

DIRECTIONS:
- Set the oven to 400 degrees.
- Place the bacon in the cast iron skillet.
- Cook over medium heat, turning occasionally, for 7 minutes.
- Drain the bacon on a paper towel.
- Remove the bacon grease from the skillet.
- Mix the garlic powder, seasoning salt, basil and oregano in a small bowl. Set aside.
- Take the pork tenderloin with the bacon strips and secure with the tooth picks per one strip of bacon.
- Slice the pork in-between bacon, and dredge the medallions in the seasoning mix.
- Melt the butter and oil in the skillet on medium heat.
- Cook each piece of pork 4 minutes on each side.
- Put the skillet in the oven and bake the pork for 17 minutes.
- Remove from the heat and let rest.
- Serve immediately and enjoy.

Slow Roasted Skillet Pork Roast

A pork roast has always been cooked in a pan in the oven. Well, the cast iron skillet gives you the freedom to roast your pork in your trailer while camping. Same great flavor in a small oven.

Prep Time: 10 minutes
Cook Time: 240 minutes
Makes: 10 Servings

INGREDIENTS:
1 boneless pork butt
1 tsp. black pepper
1 tsp. ground cumin
1 tsp. salt
½ tsp. dried thyme
1 tsp. garlic powder
½ tsp. onion powder

DIRECTIONS:
- Set the oven to 450 degrees.
- Remove the pork netting.
- Mix the spices and herbs together in a bowl.
- Rub the spice mixture all over the pork.
- Heat the skillet on high heat.
- Sear the roast on all sides. Then cover with foil.
- Place the roast in the oven and reduce the heat to 375 degrees and cook for 3 hours.
- Take off the foil and bake uncovered for another hour.
- You can serve with BBQ toppings or with tortillas.
- Serve immediately and enjoy.

VERY VEGETARIAN:

Tomato Basil Skillet Pizza

You can never go wrong with pizza! This vegetarian skillet pizza is an easy, fast dish for busy nights with the kids.

Prep Time: 5 minutes
Cook Time: 6 minutes
Makes: 4 Servings

INGREDIENTS:
1 lb. pre-made pizza dough
2 tbsp. olive oil
2 cup pizza sauce
2 cups mozzarella cheese, shredded
2 cups fresh basil, torn

DIRECTIONS:
- Divide your premade dough in half.
- Lightly flour the counter and then roll on half of the dough into a circle smaller than the skillet.
- Heat the olive oil on medium high heat.
- Place the circular dough on the skillet and cook for 1 minute.
- Flip the dough with a spatula.
- Top with the sauce, cheese and the basil.
- Cover the skillet and reduce the heat to medium.
- Cook the pizza for 5 minutes.
- Transfer to a cutting board and let cool before slicing.
- Serve immediately and enjoy.

Skillet Corn Casserole

Corn is usually served on a cob, in something or by itself. This recipe turns corn into a culinary creation.

Prep Time: 25 minutes
Cook Time: 60 minutes
Makes: 12 Servings

INGREDIENTS:

2 tbsp. butter, unsalted
1 large white onion, diced
1 small bell pepper, diced
2 tbsp. sugar
½ cup fresh sage, chopped
1 tbsp. salt
1 ¼ tsp. sweet paprika

1/8 tsp. cayenne
15 oz. frozen corn kernels
½ cup yellow cornmeal
3 large eggs
1 ¼ cups milk
½ cup heavy cream
1 cup cheddar cheese, shredded

DIRECTIONS:

- Set the oven to 350 degrees.
- Heat butter in the skillet over medium heat.
- Add the onion, bell pepper, sugar, sage, salt, paprika, and cayenne.
- Cook until onions are soft for about 10 minutes.
- Add the corn, and continue stirring for 10 minutes.
- Stir in cornmeal and remove from the heat.
- In a small bowl, mix eggs, milk, and cream and then combine the corn mixture.
- Stir to combine and sprinkle with the cheese.
- Put the skillet in the oven and bake for 20 minutes.
- Then turn on the broiler and broil for 2 minutes until brown.
- Remove and let cool.
- Serve immediately and enjoy.

Tomato and Caprese Grilled Cheese

They say that you can take any burger or sandwich and make it into a salad. Well, we took one of our favorite salads and made it into a sandwich. All we can say is Yum!

Prep Time: 5 minutes
Cook Time: 11 minutes
Makes: 4 Servings

INGREDIENTS:

8 slices sourdough bread
¼ cup basil pesto
8 oz. fresh mozzarella cheese cut in ¼ thick slices
2 large tomatoes, sliced
2 tbsp. olive oil

DIRECTIONS:

- Set the oven to 250 degrees.
- Heat the skillet on medium heat on the stove.
- Spread the presto evenly on each slice of bread.
- Distribute the mozzarella over 4 pieces of the sourdough bread.
- Top with tomatoes.
- Top the remaining pieces of bread on the sandwiches, pesto-side down.
- Brush olive oil evenly on the outside of the sandwiches and place the sandwiches (2 at a time) in the skillet.
- Cook until the bottom is toasted for 2 minutes.
- Use a flat spatula and gently press down on each sandwich. Flip and cook until the second side is toasted for 2 more minutes.
- Place the sandwiches on a baking sheet and then cook the other two sandwiches on the stove.
- Bake all four sandwiches in the oven for 7 minutes.
- Serve immediately and enjoy.

Bean and Cheese Skillet Quesadillas

Beans and cheese make for a great meal, either by themselves or in-between a tortilla.

Prep Time: 5 minutes
Cook Time: 13 minutes
Makes: 4 Servings

INGREDIENTS:

1 cup vegetarian refried beans
2 cups Monterey Jack and Cheddar Cheese Blend
4 large flour tortillas
½ tsp. chili powder

1 garlic clove, chopped
1 bag baby spinach
1 tsp. olive oil
Salt, to taste

Toppings:
Salsa
Guacamole

Sour Cream
Mexican Hot Sauce

DIRECTIONS:

- Heat oil in the skillet on medium heat.
- Put the spinach and garlic in the skillet and cook for 3 minutes.
- Next, add the chili powder and season with salt. Cook for 2 minutes until all liquid is gone.
- Transfer to a strainer and make sure that all spinach is liquid free. Set aside
- Place tortillas on the counter and spread ¼ of the beans over half of each tortilla.
- Divide the cheese over the beans and mi together. Do the same to the spinach.
- Fold each tortilla in half.
- Reheat the skillet for 3 minutes over medium heat.
- Place two of the quesadillas in the skillet and cook for 3 minutes on each side.
- Remove and place on a cutting board. Repeat with the other two.
- Cut the quesadillas into wedges and top with all of your favorite toppings.
- Serve immediately and enjoy.

A.J. Luigi

Cast Iron Skillet Brussels Sprouts Orecchiette

Tired of your normal Brussel sprouts recipe? Make the Brussel sprout the leader in this vegetarian dish.

Prep Time: 10 minutes
Cook Time: 25 minutes
Makes: 6 Servings

INGREDIENTS:

Sauce:

2 tbsp. olive oil
3 garlic cloves, minced
1 15 oz. can of whole coconut milk
½ cup yeast

1 tbsp. fresh lemon juice
1 tsp. dried basil
1 tsp. dried rosemary
Cayenne, to taste

Dish:

2 lbs. Brussel sprouts
4 tbsp. olive oil
1 ½ tbsp. White wine vinegar

2 cups orecchiette
Water, for cooking
Salt, for cooking

DIRECTIONS:

- Sauce: in a small skillet, heat the olive oil to medium heat.
- Sauté the garlic for 5 minutes.
- Add the garlic, coconut milk, yeast, lemon juice and seasonings in a blender. Blend until mixed well. Set aside.
- Brussel Sprouts: Remove the leaves and rinse the sprouts. Chop about ¼' off the base of the sprout and then cut in half.
- Pasta: Boil water and salt in a large pot.
- Heat 4 tablespoons of olive oil in the Cast Iron Skillet.
- Place the Brussel sprouts face down in the skillet and cook for 5 minutes.
- Add the white wine and stir the Brussel sprouts and cook for 10 minutes until they are tender. Leave in the pan and remove from the stove.
- The pasta and Brussel sprouts will finish at the same time. Drain the pasta and set aside. Pour the sauce into the skillet and then add the pasta.
- Turn the heat back to the medium and stir until everything is mixed and hot.
- Serve immediately with herbs and Parmesan. Enjoy.

Vegan Hamburger Helper

Who needs meat with their hamburger helper? This vegan recipe has all the flavors of a great main dish that you will forget how healthy it is for you.

Prep Time: 25 minutes
Cook Time: 15 minutes
Makes: 4 Servings

INGREDIENTS:
2 cups elbow macaroni
8 oz. organic tempeh
1 tbsp. extra virgin olive oil
1 cup marinara sauce
1 ½ cup vegan cheese sauce
1 ¼ tsp. paprika
1 ¼ tsp cumin
2 tsp. parsley
1 red bell pepper, diced
½ yellow onion, diced
1 cup green onions, diced
Salt, to taste
Pepper, to taste

DIRECTIONS:
- Prepare the vegan cheese sauce according to package.
- Dice the tempeh into small pieces and pour in the skillet with the olive oil.
- Add the marinara sauce and the spices.
- In a separate pot, cook the pasta according to the package directions.
- When pasta is complete add 2 cups of the tempeh mixture and 1 ½ cups of the cheese, onion, green onions and the red bell pepper together.
- Mix and cook for 5 minutes on medium heat.
- Serve immediately and enjoy.

SUCCULENT SIDES:

Spinach and Potato Hash

This skillet has meal doesn't need eggs to make it pop. The combination of bell peppers, onions, potatoes and spinach makes this hash the greatest addition to any main dish.

Prep Time: 30 minutes
Cook Time: 40 minutes
Makes: 4 Servings

INGREDIENTS:
6 thick bacon slices
2 medium size potatoes, peeled and chopped
1 white onion, chopped
1 red bel pepper, chopped
1 ½ tsp. garlic, chopped
1 tsp. salt
1 tsp. pepper
4 cups baby spinach
Hot Sauce, to taste
Eggs, optional

DIRECTIONS:
- Put the bacon in the cast iron skillet and cook for 12 minutes over medium heat.
- Remember to turn the bacon often.
- Remove the bacon from the pan and set aside.
- Add the potatoes, onions, and bell pepper to the skillet and cook with the bacon grease.
- Cover and cook for 5 minutes, until the potatoes are soft.
- Then uncover, and continue stirring for 5 more minutes.
- Sprinkle in the salt, pepper and garlic.
- Cook for 2 minutes and stir. Then repeat 5 times.
- Cut or crumble the bacon and spinach. Pour over the top and mix.
- Take the skillet off the heat and cook for 2 minutes until the spinach wilts.
- Serve immediately with hot sauce and enjoy. Add eggs to make it a full meal.

One Cast Iron Skillet Zesty Salsa

Tired of the same old salsa selections at the store? Nothing is better than the smell of fresh salsa at home. Refrigerate for up to 3 days and you can spoon this on top of everything.

Prep Time: 10 minutes
Cook Time: 20 minutes
Makes: 4 Servings

INGREDIENTS:

3 big plum tomatoes, halved
2 garlic cloves, unpeeled
1 jalapeno, halved and deseeded
1 medium sized white onion, diced
2 tbsp. lime juice
¾ tsp. salt
1/3 cup cilantro, chopped

DIRECTIONS:

- Heat the skillet over medium for 5 minutes.
- Put the tomatoes in the skillet, skin side up, and then add the garlic and jalapeno pepper.
- Cook for 6 minutes stirring often.
- Pour the mixture into a blender.
- Peel the garlic and put in blender.
- Cook the onions in the skillet and cook for 6 minutes and then pour in with the tomato mixture.
- Turn on the blender for 40 seconds.
- Add the cilantro and salt and process until smooth.
- Cool for 10 minutes.
- Serve immediately with tortilla chips and enjoy.

Creamy Chicken Soup Mac & Cheese

There are so many ways to make this classic dish, and we came up with a new one. The creaminess of the chicken soup gives this side dish the feel of chicken, but lets it stand on its own.

Prep Time: 20 minutes
Cook Time: 25 minutes
Makes: 6 Servings

INGREDIENTS:
1 can cream of chicken soup
2 tbsp. butter
1 medium red onion, diced
1 green bell pepper, diced
1 can diced tomatoes and green chilies
1 package Kraft or Velveeta cheese, cubed
½ cup sour cream
1 ¼ tsp. chili powder
½ tsp. ground cumin
2 cups cheddar cheese, shredded
½ package cellentani pasta

DIRECTIONS:
- Set the oven to 350 degrees.
- Prepare the pasta according to the package.
- Heat and melt the butter in the cast iron skillet over medium-high heat.
- Pour in the onion and bell pepper and sauté for 5 minutes.
- Next, slowly stir in the tomatoes and green chilies and Kraft cheese.
- Cook for 2 minutes.
- Add in the rest of the ingredients (besides the cheddar cheese), and the hot pasta in the skillet until fully mixed.
- Sprinkle the cheddar cheese on top and bake for 30 minutes.
- Serve immediately with short braised ribs and enjoy.

Skillet Fried Okra

Fried okra is a staple in the south. Smother them in a pecan batter and you have a winner. Eat alongside some roasted chicken or fish and you have yourself a great meal.

Prep Time: 10 minutes
Cook Time: 16 minutes
Makes: 8 Servings

INGREDIENTS:
1 cup pecans
1 1.2 cups baking mix
1 tsp. salt
1 tsp. pepper
2 packages frozen whole okra, thawed
Peanut Oil, for frying

DIRECTIONS:
- Set the oven to 350 degrees.
- Place the pecans on a baking sheet and bake for 10 minutes.
- Pour the pecans, baking mix, salt and pepper into a blender and ground finely.
- In a large bowl, pour in the pecan mixture and toss the okra in it.
- In the cast iron skillet pour 2 inches of peanut oil and heat to 350 degrees.
- Fry the okra in batches for 6 minutes until golden brown.
- Drain and place on a paper towel.
- Serve immediately and enjoy.

Honeyed White Turnips

Who said turnips had to be bland? This honey and apple cider turnip recipe will change how you feel about turnips forever.

Prep Time: 5 minutes
Cook Time: 30 minutes
Makes: 4 Servings

INGREDIENTS:
15 small white turnips
3 tbsp. butter
3 tbsp. apple cider vinegar
1 tbsp. salt
1 tbsp. pepper
2 tbsp. honey

DIRECTIONS:
- Heat the cast iron skillet over medium heat for 5 minutes.
- Start by trimming the turnips and cut in half.
- Melt 2 tbsp. of butter in the skillet and place the turnips in the skillet, skin side up.
- Cook for 4 minutes.
- Pour the vinegar on top and add ¼ inch of water.
- Season with salt.
- Let the turnips boil, and then cover and simmer for 5 minutes on medium low heat.
- Uncover and bring back to a boil for 4 minutes.
- Once water is almost completely gone, cook for 8 more minutes, stirring occasionally.
- When water has full evaporated, stir in the honey and the remaining butter.
- Serve immediately and enjoy.

Skillet Garlic Sweet Potatoes

Forget the marshmallows and brown sugar. The garlic and rosemary will have you making this recipe every holiday.

Prep Time: 30 minutes
Cook Time: 30 minutes
Makes: 4 Servings

INGREDIENTS:
3 medium sweet potatoes
1 large sprig rosemary
1 large sprig thyme
3 tbsp. butter, unsalted
2 tbsp. olive oil
2 garlic cloves, minced
¼ tbsp. nutmeg
Salt, to taste
Pepper, to taste

DIRECTIONS:
- Set the oven to 425 degrees.
- Thinly slice the sweet potatoes leaving the skin on.
- Form the slices of sweet potatoes in a circle in the cast iron skillet.
- Place the rosemary and thyme underneath or between 5 slices of sweet potato.
- Melt the butter and oil in small pot.
- Toss in the garlic, and the salt and pepper.
- Add in the nutmeg and stir.
- Pour the mixture over the potatoes and bake for 45 minutes.
- Serve immediately and enjoy.

BRING HOME BREAKFAST:

Egg and Tater Tot Breakfast Pizza

Eggs and tater tots on pizza? Why not? Instead of eating cold leftover pizza for breakfast, make this your go to breakfast pizza.

Prep Time: 30 minutes
Cook Time: 20 minutes
Makes: 4 Servings

INGREDIENTS:

1 lb. pre-made pizza dough
2 tbsp. olive oil
5 slices of provolone cheese
1 cup tater tots, baked
4 slices of Applewood smoked bacon, cooked and diced

4 slices Canadian bacon, diced
3 large eggs
Salt, to taste
Pepper, to taste
Fresh chives, for garnish
Fresh thyme, for garnish

DIRECTIONS:

- Set the oven to 450 degrees.
- Let the dough sit out for 30 minutes.
- Pour 1 tsp. olive oil in the cast iron skillet and place the dough on top of it.
- Form the dough into a disk shape using your hand.
- Then, stretch the dough out from the center and form it all around the inside of the skillet.
- Let it rest for 5 minutes.
- Coat the top of the dough with the remaining tsp. of olive oil.
- Top with cheese slices, Canadian bacon, and bacon.
- When putting tater tots on, arrange so there is room for the cracked eggs.
- Cook on high heat for 4 minutes
- Remove and crack eggs on top of the pizza.
- Season with salt and pepper.
- Bake in the oven for 10 minutes.
- Let cook. Then transfer to cutting board and slice.
- Serve immediately and enjoy.

Easy Weekday Morning Skillet Breakfast

Need to make breakfast in a hurry? This three-ingredient skillet breakfast might become part of your everyday routine.

Prep Time: 2 minutes
Cook Time: 15 minutes
Makes: 2 Servings

INGREDIENTS:
1 lb. ground beef
1 cup salsa
6 eggs

DIRECTIONS:
- Heat oil in the skillet over medium heat for 5 minutes.
- Place the ground beef in the skillet and cook for 5 minutes or until it browns.
- Combine the salsa and let cook for 3 minutes.
- Crack the eggs in the skillet and cover.
- Cook for 7 minutes. Sprinkle cheese over the top if desired.
- Serve immediately and enjoy.

Berry Skillet Cakes

Make this your new Saturday morning favorite. Folding the berries inside the batter gives the cakes a sweetness that you will remember for a lifetime.

Prep Time: 5 minutes
Cook Time: 10 minutes
Makes: 2 Servings

INGREDIENTS:

1 ¼ cups flour
2 tsp. baking powder
1 tsp. salt
2 tbsp. sugar
1 egg
1 cup milk
½ cup strawberries, chopped
½ cup blueberries, halved
1 tsp. vegetable oil

Toppings:
Whipped Cream
Butter
Maple Syrup

DIRECTIONS:
- Mix the flour, baking powder, salt and sugar together.
- Stir in the egg with the mil.
- Slowly add in the strawberries and blueberries.
- Heat the cast iron skillet with olive oil.
- Pour ½ cup of the batter into the skillet to form a cake. You can make more than one at a time if comfortable.
- Flip when dry on the opposite side and cook until golden brown.
- Serve immediately with the toppings of your choice and enjoy.

The Best Scrambled Egg Recipe

There is no wrong way to make scrambled eggs you say. Wrong. This is the right way! I guarantee it.

Prep Time: 1 minute
Cook Time: 5 minutes
Makes: 1 Serving

INGREDIENTS:
2 tsp. coconut oil
2 eggs
2 tbsp. milk
¼ cup cheddar cheese, shredded
Salt, to taste
Pepper, to taste
Green onion, sliced

DIRECTIONS:
- Heat 1 tsp. of coconut oil in the cast iron skillet over medium low heat.
- Pour the rest of the coconut oil in the pan to coat it.
- In a separate bowl, whisk the eggs and milk together.
- Pour into the skillet and let cook for 20 seconds to start thickening.
- Push them around with a spatula until they reach the desired consistency.
- Remove from the heat and transfer to a plate.
- Top with salt, pepper, cheese and garnish.
- Serve immediately and enjoy.

Cinnamon-Vanilla French toast

You can never go wrong with baked and oven toasted French toast. Drizzle some maple syrup and powdered sugar on top and you will wonder why you never used cinnamon and vanilla before.

Prep Time: 10 minutes
Cook Time: 20 minutes
Makes: 4 Servings

INGREDIENTS:

6 slices French bread, thick
1 tbsp. butter
2 eggs
½ cup mile
1 tsp. vanilla extract
½ tsp. ground cinnamon
½ tsp. ground nutmeg
¼ tsp. ground allspice
1 tsp. salt

DIRECTIONS:

- Set the oven to 400 degrees.
- Mix milk, vanilla, salt, spices and eggs together in a large bowl.
- Soak bread pieces in the mixture.
- Heat the cast iron skillet over medium heat.
- Melt the butter.
- Cook the toast in batches. Each piece cooks for 3 minutes per each side.
- When done, transfer the bread to a baking sheet and toast for 15 minutes.
- Serve immediately with powdered sugar or maple syrup and enjoy.

Hearty Breakfast Casserole

This recipe pairs all of the best meats, and vegetable ingredients together. Now all you have to decide is what meal you want to make this for.

Prep Time: 30 minutes
Cook Time: 55 minutes
Makes: 4 Servings

INGREDIENTS:
10 slices of apple-wood smoked bacon
5 red potatoes, diced
1 red bell pepper, diced
1 orange bell pepper, diced
½ red onion, diced
1 jalapeno, diced and seeded
1 cup cheddar cheese, shredded
6 eggs
¾ cup milk
1 tbs. garlic salt
1 tbsp. pepper
1 tsp. salt
1 tsp. paprika

DIRECTIONS:
- Set the oven to 425 degrees.
- Cook the bacon in the cast iron skillet for 10 minutes over medium heat.
- Drain the bacon and crumble.
- In the same skillet, layer the potatoes, bell peppers, onion and jalapeno.
- Sprinkle half of the cheese on the top and toss the bacon bits over the cheese.
- Combine the eggs, milk, and garlic salt, pepper, salt and paprika together and pour over the potato mixture.
- Bake for 35 minutes.
- Remove from oven and top with the rest of the cheese.
- Cook for another 10 minutes until the cheese is melted.
- Serve immediately and enjoy.

DELICIOUS DESSERTS:

One Stop Skillet S'mores Graham Cracker Dip

This is the perfect way to celebrate summer all year long. With the One Stop Skillet S'mores Graham Cracker Dip, you and your family can enjoy the feel of camping right in your living room.

Prep Time: 5 minutes
Cook Time: 6 minutes
Makes: 6 Servings

INGREDIENTS:
4 Hershey's Milk Chocolate Bars
1 box of Graham crackers
1 bag of large Marshmallows

DIRECTIONS:
- Set the oven to 450 degrees.
- Coat the Cast Iron Skillet with cooking spray
- Layer the bottom of the skillet with the chocolate bars.
- Then cover with a layer of marshmallows.
- Bake for 7 minutes or until the marshmallows are toasted.
- Cool for 10 minutes
- Serve immediately, dip with the graham crackers and enjoy.

Peanut Buttery Reese's Nachos

This peanut butter and chocolate mixture will have you grabbing for the milk, and for another piece.

Prep Time: 10 minutes
Cook Time: 10 minutes
Makes: 6 Servings

INGREDIENTS:
¼ cup chocolate, melted
6 Reese's Peanut Butter Cups, chopped
1 packet Reese's Pieces
1 cup Marshmallows, mini
¼ cup peanut butter, hot
20 graham crackers, broken into pieces

DIRECTIONS:
- Set the oven to 300 degrees.
- Coat the bottom of the Cast Iron Skillet with cooking spray or oil.
- Start layering the skillet with graham crackers, Reese's cups and pieces, and marshmallows.
- Drizzle the chocolate and peanut butter on top.
- Place in oven and bake for 10 minutes or until the marshmallows are toasted.
- Serve immediately and enjoy.

One Size Skillet Toffee Brownie

You can never go wrong with the gooey, chocolateness of a brownie. In this recipe, we pair the brownie with toffee pieces that give it a little bit of a crunch.

Prep Time: 15 minutes
Cook Time: 30 minutes
Makes: 5 Servings

INGREDIENTS:
1 stick, unsalted butter
4 oz. chocolate chips
½ cup chocolate chips
1 ½ oz. unsweetened chocolate
2 large eggs
1 ½ tsp. vanilla extract
1.2 cup sugar
¼ cup all-purpose flour
1 tbsp. all-purpose flour
1 tsp. baking powder
¼ tsp. salt
½ cup toffee pieces

DIRECTIONS:
- Set the oven to 350 degrees.
- In a large bowl, melt butter, 4 oz. chocolate chips & chocolate till smooth.
- Set aside and cool for 15 minutes.
- In a separate bowl, mix the eggs, vanilla and sugar together. Stir in the chocolate mixture until combined.
- In another bowl, mix the baking powder, ¼ cup flour and salt together.
- Stir in the chocolate mixture until mixed thoroughly.
- In another bowl, mix the remaining chocolate chips, toffee bits, and flour together. Mix with the chocolate mixture.
- Pour the batter into the cast iron skillet and place on a baking sheet.
- Bake for 30 minutes.
- Serve immediately with vanilla ice cream, hot fudge, and more toffee pieces and enjoy.

A.J. Luigi

Caramel Giant Cinnamon Roll

Go big or go home right? We promise that this Giant Caramel Cinnamon Roll will not disappoint. We won't tell anyone if you decide to eat it in one sitting. We know it's that good!

Prep Time: 20 minutes
Cook Time: 30 minutes
Makes: 8 Servings

INGREDIENTS:

Pears:
2 tbsp. butter
¼ cup brown sugar
2 large pears, cored and diced

Cinnamon Roll:
2 can Pillsbury Buttermilk Biscuits
½ cup brown sugar
1 tsp. cinnamon
1 tsp. nutmeg
¼ cup butter, melted

Vanilla Icing:
1 cup powdered sugar
2 tbsp. milk
1 tsp. vanilla extract

DIRECTIONS:
- Set the oven to 350 degrees. Heat the cast iron skillet over medium heat.
- Melt the butter in the skillet, add the brown sugar, stirring for 1 minute.
- Add the pears and toss with the sugar. Cook for 8 minutes until brown.
- Remove the pears and let cook.
- In a small bowl, mix the ½ cup of brown sugar, cinnamon, and nutmeg.
- Roll each biscuit, brush with the melted butter and sprinkle with the cinnamon mixture. Cut each biscuit into 3 long strips with a pizza cutter.
- Roll up one strip in the center of the skillet and surround with the pears. Repeat this until all the dough is surrounded by pears. Bake 30 minutes.
- Mix all the icing ingredients together.
- Take the cinnamon roll out of the oven and let cool.
- Drizzle with the icing and serve immediately and enjoy.

Gooey Chocolatey Texas Skillet Cake

This recipe has always been a go to for big parties or events. Well, now you can make this recipe without all of the leftovers.

Prep Time: 5 minutes
Cook Time: 30 minutes
Makes: 8 Servings

INGREDIENTS:

½ all-purpose flour
¾ tsp. baking soda
1 1.4 cup sugar
½ tsp. salt
¾ stick butter, unsalted
1.4 cup canola oil

2 tbsp. canola oil
¼ cup unsweetened cocoa powder
¾ cup water
½ cup buttermilk
2 eggs
1 tsp. vanilla extract

Frosting:
1 stick butter, unsalted
2 tbsp. unsweetened cocoa powder
¼ cup milk

½ cup toasted pecans, chopped
2 cups powdered sugar
½ tsp. vanilla extract

DIRECTIONS:

- Set the oven to 350 degrees.
- Start by mixing the flour, baking soda, sugar and salt in a mixing bowl and set aside.
- Heat the cast iron skillet on the stove on high heat for 5 minutes.
- Bring the butter, canola oil, cocoa powder and water to a boil.
- Remove from the heat and mix in all of the dry ingredients, along with the buttermilk, egg, and vanilla. Then bake in the oven for 25 minutes.
- Remove and let cook.
- Place a small pan on the stove and boil the butter, cocoa and milk over medium heat.
- Remove from the heat and mix in the powdered sugar, pecans and vanilla. Mix until smooth. Pour the cake and spread evenly.
- Let rest for 10 minutes. Serve immediately with vanilla ice cream and enjoy.

Brown Sugar and Butterscotch Skillet Pumpkin Pie

Who would think to mess with a classic? Someone who would like to score points with mom during their next holiday get together. This Pie will make everyone's mouth drool.

Prep Time: 30 minutes
Cook Time: 60 minutes
Makes: 4 Servings

INGREDIENTS:

1 store bough crust, pre-baked
6 tbsp. butter, unsalted
1 cup brown sugar
2 tbsp. water
½ cup heavy cream
½ cup vanilla extract
2 large eggs
2 large egg yolks
½ tsp. salt

1 2/3 cups pumpkin puree
¾ tsp. ground allspice
¾ tsp. ground cinnamon
¾ tsp. ground nutmeg
¼ tsp. ginger
1/8 tsp. ground cloves
1 tsp. molasses
3 tsp. lemon juice
2/3 cup milk

DIRECTIONS:

- Set the oven to 350 degrees.
- Heat the cast iron skillet on the stove over medium heat.
- Melt the butter in the skillet until brown.
- Stir in the brown sugar, and slowly add in the water.
- Boil the mixture and simmer until it reaches 225 degrees.
- Remove from heat and carefully add the heavy cream until smooth.
- Cool for 10 minutes and then add in the vanilla.
- Combine the salt, eggs and egg yolks in a bowl and set aside.
- Blend the pumpkin puree, allspice, cinnamon, nutmeg, ginger, cloves, molasses and lemon juice until smooth.
- Turn the blender on low and slowly pour in the butterscotch that was set aside. Then stir in the egg mixture and the milk. Blend until smooth.
- Strain the filling into a separate bowl by using a mesh sieve.
- Place the pie crust in the cast iron skillet and pour the mixture on top.
- Bake for 55 minutes. When done, allow to cool for 3 hours.

NEXT UP ON THE LIST!

Show Us Some Love... ☺

PLEASE LEAVE US AN AMAZON REVIEW!

If you were pleased with our book then leave us a review on Amazon where you purchased this book! Simply, scroll to the bottom & review!

>>> www.Amazon.com/dp/B07HRY9K6V <<<

In the world of an author who writes books independently, your reviews are not only touching but important so that we know you like the material we have prepared for "you" our audience! So, leave us a review...we would love to see that you enjoyed our book!

If for any reason that you were less than happy with your experience then send me an email at **Info@RecipeNerds.com** and let me know how we can better your experience. We always come out with a few volumes of our books and will possibly be able to address some of your concerns. Do keep in mind that we strive to do our best to give you the highest quality of what "we the independent authors" pour our heart and tears into.

Hello all...I am very excited that you have purchased one of my publications. Please feel free to give us an amazon review where you purchased the book! If you already have, then I thank you for your many great reviews and comments! With a warm heart! ~Sarah Conner "Personal & Professional Chef"

A.J. Luigi

YOURS FOR LOOKING

"BONUS" Get Your Marinades for Meats & Veggies!

Get your very own Air Fryer Marinade Quick Start Guide! This quick start guide will show you how to get the best tasting foods when cooking from your air fryer! **GET YOURS NOW** by just simply clicking the button below! **Enjoy!**

http://eepurl.com/dzsApr

Metric Volume, metric weight and oven temperature charts are tools that everyone wants in the kitchen, but are never around when you need them. That's why we have created these charts for you so you never skip a beat when you're cooking! Hope this helps! :)

Metric Volume Conversions Chart

US Volume Measure	Metric Equivalent
1/8 teaspoon	0.5 milliliters
1/4 teaspoon	1 milliliter
1/2 teaspoon	2.5 milliliters
3/4 teaspoon	4 milliliters
1 teaspoon	5 milliliters
1 1/4 teaspoons	6 milliliters
1 1/2 teaspoons	7.5 milliliters
1 3/4 teaspoons	8.5 milliliters
2 teaspoons	10 milliliters
1/2 tablespoon	7.5 milliliters
1 tbsp. (3 teaspoons, 1/2 fluid ounce)	15 milliliters
2 tbsp. (1 fluid ounce)	30 milliliters
1/4 cup (4 tablespoons)	60 milliliters
1/3 cup	90 milliliters
1/2 cup (4 fluid ounces)	125 milliliters
2/3 cup	160 milliliters
3/4 cup (6 fluid ounces)	180 milliliters
1 cup (16 tablespoons, 8 fluid ounces)	250 milliliters
1 1/4 cups	300 milliliters
1 1/2 cups (12 fluid ounces)	360 milliliters
1 2/3 cups	400 milliliters
2 cups (1 pint)	500 Milliliters
3 cups	700 Milliliters
4 cups (1 quart)	950 milliliters
1 quart plus 1/4 cup	1 liter
4 quarts (1 gallon)	3.8 liters

Metric Weight Conversion Chart

US Weight Measure	Metric Equivalent
1/2 ounce	7 grams
1/2 ounce	15 grams
3/4 ounce	21 grams
1 ounce	28 grams
1 1/4 ounces	35 grams
1 1/2 ounces	42.5 grams
1 2/3 ounces	45 grams
2 ounces	57 grams
3 ounces	85 grams
4 oz. (1/4 lb.)	113 grams
5 ounces	142 grams
6 ounces	170 grams
7 ounces	198 grams
8 oz. (1/2 lb.)	227 grams
12 oz. (3/4 lb.)	340 Grams
16 oz. (1 lb.)	454 grams
32.5 oz. (2.2 lbs.)	1 kilogram

Temperature Conversion Chart

Degrees Fahrenheit	Degrees Celsius	Cool to Hot
200° F	100° C	Very cool oven
250° F	120° C	Very cool oven
275° F	140° C	Cool oven
300° F	150° C	Cool oven
325° F	160° C	Very moderate oven
350° F	180° C	Moderate oven
375° F	190° C	Moderate oven
400° F	200° C	Moderately hot oven
425° F	220° C	Hot oven
450° F	230° C	Hot oven
475° F	246° C	Very hot oven

ABOUT THE AUTHOR

A.J. Luigi is a Professional Gourmet Italian Chef that has over 25 years of experience in his craft as a Chef. He moved to the States as a young boy and created a passion for cooking for his large family! From this experience, he has created this special recipe book just for you! These special recipes within this book are some of his very own personal favorites that he has shared with you, his audience. His profession calls for her to visit many well-known names to cater special events and whip up some of the best dishes he can offer. In his spare time, he enjoys travel, walks on the beach and perfecting his craft, creating new and delicious recipes, with you in mind! Enjoy!

"Thank you for your purchase of my book! Hoping it captures your and heart gives you many ideas to create some of what you can come up with from this Cast Iron Skillet book! Enjoy!"

With a warm heart...

A.J. Luigi, Professional Chef

Cast Iron Skillet Secret Recipe Creations & Notes:

Create your very own "Marvelous Masterpieces". Log all of your new recipes in this recipe log section. You'll be amazed on how many ideas you come up with! **Now get creating!**

Recipe Name	Temp.	Time	Special Ingredients

Made in the USA
Lexington, KY
30 November 2018